HILLWALK
NORTH SNOWDONIA

**29 One-day Walks in the Mountains
of North-west Wales**

DAVID HERMAN

Gwasg Carreg Gwalch

'Would you be so kind as to tell me which way I should go', said Alice.
'That depends to a great extent on where you want to get to', said the cat.
'I don't know exactly', said Alice.
'Then it doesn't matter which way you go either', said the cat.

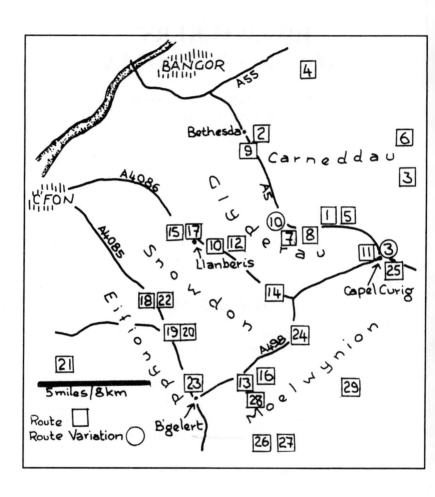

The Routes

ABOUT THIS BOOK

This is a book of walking routes; it tries to cover the best of all the mountain areas of North Snowdonia in enjoyable circuits. It does not concern itself with getting to the summits just for the sake of doing so, so I did not set out to climb every summit over 3000ft, 1000m or any other arbitrary height.

I have not included the Bristly Ridge, the north face of Tryfan and Crib Goch among the routes for the simple reason that they are much more scrambling than walking routes and even more to the point, though I have climbed two of them in the past I am far too scared to attempt them now, still less describe them with any confidence. However, I have somewhat illogically included an easy route up Tryfan since it is fine summit and it certainly does not present anything like the difficulties of the other three climbs.

You might note that I do not describe every route as being superbly attractive. I have taken a 'warts and all' approach, but this does not mean that I consider some of the routes not worth doing. In my opinion they all most certainly are.

The book also describes in brief two looped walking routes – one five-day, one six – based on overnighting in youth hostels, a fine way of getting to know North Snowdonia and with the added attraction of ending up in a congenial – a different congenial – place every night. And since Snowdonia is not always blessed with fine, sunny days, I have included a few low-level routes that you might tackle should the weather preclude the high mountains.

It hardly needs to be said that there are many years of enjoyable walking to be had in North Snowdonia and this book is only a small sample of what's there. After you have completed some of the routes given here go out and explore for yourself: you are unlikely to be disappointed.

I wish you many happy days exploring the mountains of North Snowdonia!

David Herman

A FIRST LOOK AROUND

There are five groups of mountains in North Snowdonia, separated by major roads. These ranges are briefly described here, roughly from north to south.

The Carneddau (routes 1-6)

This is the area north and east of the A5, falling gently on the north to the coast and on the east to the fertile Dyffryn Conwy. This extensive range of high country consists for the most part of undulating moorland, diversified here and there by mountain lakes and valleys and by startlingly unexpected castles of rocks. To the south the hills assume a more rugged aspect with the highest summits at Llywelyn (1064m) and Dafydd (1044m), which are joined by a fine ridge. Running south-east of Llywelyn is a rocky ridge with one spectacular bwlch (pass). The ridge runs beyond this into a rugged, cliff- and crag-bound area around Llyn Cowlyd Reservoir and then into lower wooded country around Betws-y-coed.

The Glyderau/Glyders (routes 7-12)

The Glyderau lie between the A5 and the A4086. This highly rewarding range runs in a distinct L-shape from north to east. It falls in magnificent cwms and cliffs on these two sides while the western and southern flanks are comparatively tame. The short central section, from the steep rise south-west to Glyder Fawr (999m) as far as the drop east of Glyder Fach (994m) is the heart of the range, a region of shattered rock, stretches of scree and mounds of boulders. Cradled by the central section is the isolated, highly distinctive peak of Tryfan (915m).

To the north of this central section, culminating in lofty Y Garn (947m), the eastward-falling cliffs are particularly impressive. To the central section's east the range peters out somewhat towards Capel Curig.

The Snowdon Group (routes 13-18)
Between the A4086, the A498 and the A4085 is the Snowdon Group, a complex set of mountains culminating (unsurprisingly) in Snowdon/Yr Wyddfa itself, at 1085m the highest mountain in Wales. Because of the rack railway to it, its summit is a mecca for the day-tripper. This is a most popular walking area with well-used (and indeed over-used) paths reaching the summit.

Several spurs overlooking fine cliffs and cwms run in most directions except west from Snowdon and its satellite peaks, of which the formidable Crib Goch is the best known, but there are others of which those towards Y Lliwedd (898m) and Yr Aran (747m) are also spectacular. The west side of the main range is mostly gently sloped moorland, though Cwm Clogwyn is quite splendid.

Eifionydd (routes 19-23)
This area to the west of the A498 and the A4085 contains a fine horseshoe of peaks grouped around the long valley of Cwm Pennant of which the exhilarating Nantlle Ridge, 7km long and reaching 734m high, is the centre-point. The highest and most prominent peak is Moel Hebog (782m), the climax of a fine walk. This area also includes the small isolated hills north of the B4418.

Moelwynion (routes 24-29)
This group east and south of the A4086 and the A498 is a diverse, rumpled area, though marred by numerous abandoned and working slate mines. It rises to 872m at the long, isolated ridge of Moel Siabod and also includes distinctive and rocky Cnicht (689m), to the west of the improbably straight valley of Cwm Croesor. In addition there are rewarding if little walked areas with rugged outcrops around Moelwyn Mawr and Bach (770m and 710m) and the maze of lakes close to Moel Druman (698m).

LOCAL TOWNS
The most convenient large towns in the area are undoubtedly **Bangor** and **Caernarfon** to the north. Both have excellent facilities and are good centres for public transport, an important consideration if you are relying on it. Nearer the mountains are popular and lively **Llanberis**, also a good centre if you are relying on buses and convenient to the Snowdon Group and the Glyderau; stylish **Betws-y-coed** and tiny **Capel Curig** at the east of the mountains; and **Bethesda**, a

quarrying town with good bus connections and close to the Carneddau and the Glyderau. Finally, touristy **Beddgelert** and tiny **Rhyd-Ddu**, both close to Eifionydd, the Snowdon Group and Moelwynion.

THE ROUTE DESCRIPTIONS

There are a few points that should be mentioned in order to make the route descriptions clearer.

Walking Time. I have taken the standard walking time to be a metricated and somewhat slower version of Naismith's Rule; the one I have used being one hour for each 4km on the flat, plus one hour for each 600m climbed. To this I have added some time to allow for difficulties such as steep descents, difficult underfoot conditions or possibly navigational uncertainties. This version of Naismith's is my idea of an average pace to maintain over a day's walking (without stops) but you may well have to adjust it depending on your own pace.

Grid References (gr). These four or six digit figures uniquely identify a location on the map, where they are fully explained.

Units. Metric units are used throughout because the maps are now exclusively metric and because there are more than enough figures in this book as it stands. (The exception is car journeys since odometers are normally in miles.) There is a rough chart inside the back cover if you are wedded to imperial.

Map. The recommended map for all but one of the walks in this book is the Ordnance Survey's 1:50 000 sheet 115, an excellent map on a suitable scale.

The Sketch Map given with each route is emphatically NOT sufficient for you to find your way round. It does however give you a rough outline and includes any small-scale features (perhaps not given on the OS map) that may be important or reassuring for navigation. These features are mentioned **in bold** in the route description. All the sketch maps are on a scale of 1:50 000. The **inset sketch maps** are not to scale but are correctly oriented (north to the top).

TAKE CARE!

The most difficult walk in good conditions could be far easier to navigate round than the easiest in bad, and it is impossible (for me anyway) to describe a route, even on paths, that will be foolproof if conditions are poor. Take precautions therefore and do not venture forth if you are not both confident and experienced for the conditions you are likely to face. Start with a navigationally easy route. Note the weather forecast before you set off and plan accordingly.

A PERSONAL ROUTE SELECTION

The following list gives one route for each of the five areas mentioned above. In each of the areas there are routes almost as good, maybe better, than these:
Route 1: The High Carneddau and Pen Yr Helgi Du;
Route 8: Y Gribin, Glyder Fach and Tryfan or Route 9 (the Northern Glyderau);
Route 14: Pen-y-Pass, Y Lliwedd and Snowdon;
Route 19: The Nantlle Ridge (my favourite in North Snowdonia);
Route 26: Cnicht from Croesor.

WEATHER

Snowdonia gets more than its fair share of rain and poor visibility. Page 61 gives you a few options in case of bad weather; otherwise take a note of the weather forecast and respond appropriately. There are forecasts on Radio 4 Wales (check current times); on the web at www.metoffice.gov.uk (among others sites) or you can phone 0870-9000-100 (national rates).

WELSH PLACE-NAMES

Not being a native, I cannot help you with the pronunciation of Welsh place-names. You should try to avoid gross errors by learning the approximate pronunciation from a book or by asking Welsh speakers.

Below I have taken some topographical words and given an English equivalent. These words will prove useful in understanding the route descriptions: in the case of those given in **bold** they are essential to know. They are:

Afon (river), Bach (small), Bont or Pont (bridge), Bryn (hill), **Bwlch** (col or pass), Coed (wood), Craig (rock), **Cwm** (cirque or corrie but also used for any mountain valley), Du (black), Dyffryn (valley), Foel or Moel (rounded or bare hill), **Llyn**, pl **Llynnau** (lake), Mawr (large), Mynydd (mountain), **Nant** (brook or rocky gorge, or any mountain valley), Pen (top), Tal (tall/at the head of).

Lastly, all the place names are spelt as on the OS maps, with a few minor exceptions where, I have been assured, the OS is incorrect. These names should however still be easily recognisable on the maps.

BUSES

With more than a little ingenuity you can organise walks in Snowdonia without a car. First get a timetable from Gwynedd county council (www.gwynedd.gov.uk). You may find it marginally easier to decipher than Linear B, so here are a few pointers.

First have a look at the Sherpa service (the ones with 'S' before the bus number) as this is a most useful service that covers all the main mountain roads in Snowdonia, though in most cases with an infrequent service. If you are doing an A to B walk (and here buses are almost indispensable if you haven't got at least two cars), then start and end on the same road, and so get the same bus; it's generally easier to get back to base that way. Lastly, use the less frequent service in the morning so you do not have to rush for that infrequent bus in the evening.

Here are some of the more useful non-Sherpa buses:

From **Bangor** to Bethesda look at routes 6 (infrequent), 7 (frequent), 66 (moderately frequent), 67 (Sundays only), 76, 77 (both moderately frequent). From Bangor to Llanberis look at routes 85, 86 (both moderately frequent). From **Caernarfon** to Nebo look at route 1A (moderately frequent). From Caernarfon to Nantlle look at route 80 (infrequent). From Caernarfon to Llanberis and Nant Peris look at route 88 (moderately frequent).

Lastly, remember also that if walking routes in this book can be done using the bus then this is noted in the route description.

ROUTE 1: THE HIGH CARNEDDAU AND PEN YR HELGI DU

A walk with great variety: in turn a steep climb to Pen yr Ole Wen, along the high ground between the two highest Carneddau peaks, and on to Pen yr Helgi Du via a fine bwlch. A quieter end: down a broad grassy spur and back on level ground along a valley floor.

Know Before You Go There are three places where mild scrambling is necessary: the first is near the start and once surmounted, you will know that that is probably as difficult as it gets. Except for the descent from the summit of Carnedd Llywelyn navigation is quite easy. There are several places where you can take an escape route.

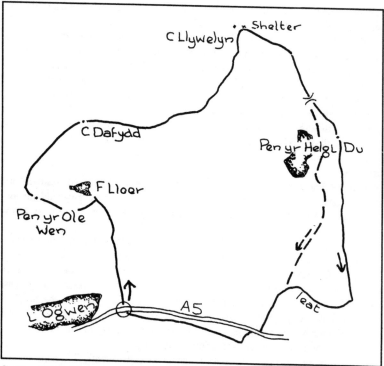

Getting There The start is on the A5 just east of Llyn Ogwen at about gr 668605. Coming from Bethesda pass Llyn Ogwen and park just after it. There is a dense copse of trees on the left here and the straight stretch of road offers plenty of parking. From Capel Curig park around this copse about 4 miles from the junction of the A4086 and the A5. **Bus:** S6 from Bethesda or Betws-y-coed.

Walking Time 5.5 hours (distance 15km, climb 1020m).

Route Take a track through the copse and immediately turn right off it to cross a stile. Turn uphill here and follow an intermittent path indicated by not very helpful yellow posts or the stream issuing from the lake Ffynnon Lloer. A stiff climb ensues to the lake, which is set in a dramatic bowl overlooked by rugged cliffs, an ample reward for your considerable efforts so far.

The idea now is to climb westward on the crest of the steep wall reaching out on the south side of the lake. The first part of this climb is the hardest, after which take the clear path all the way to the summit of the first peak, Pen yr Ole Wen (978m), its flat summit crowned by a jerry-built shelter. From here walk roughly north-east along a ridge over or around heaps of rocks to the summit of Carnedd Dafydd (1044m). Dafydd commands a wide panorama where not blocked by its slightly higher brother Llywelyn, the next target; the latter is easily reached over a narrow gently curving ridge commanding lovely views left into the long valley of the Afon Llafar. It ends in a stiff zig-zag climb through stones to the summit plateau.

Carnedd Llywelyn (1064m) is not the easiest summit to navigate from even in good weather, so as you reach the summit plateau, watch out for the **first shelter** and use this as the starting point for the descent along a spur at about 110°, cliffs on the left, many boulders underfoot. There is a path but since it eschews the best views you may prefer to keep to its left and walk the bumpy crest.

There is an unexpected and not altogether welcome surprise just before the bwlch facing the next summit, Pen yr Helgi Du (833m) – a precipitous, rocky but short drop. Below it is the narrow, dramatic and splendid bwlch overlooking Ffynnon Llugwy Reservoir on the right and the remote Cwm Eigiau on the left. If you have to, this is one place to easily shorten the route by taking a clear but tortuous path down to the reservoir and from it following the nasty paved road back to the A5.

Back on the main route scramble south-east to Pen yr Helgi Du. There is a steep path starting just to the right of the crest, this initial section being the most hazardous part. Curiously the summit itself, after the Trojan effort to get there is a tame, grassy, almost flat area with two sizable cairns, both well off the summit. From the first of these you can start your descent.

The rest of the route is without peril, but may require a little attention to navigation. Take an unnecessary path south over short grass keeping to the crest of a broad spur. Pass through a gap in a crossways wall, and continue on a clear path to a leat, a narrow contouring water channel. Turn right at the leat to the straight boring road already mentioned and take it down to the A5. Turn right here, turn left shortly into a camping site and right at the gate 'Caseg Fraith' to follow track and path to the start. A pleasant, gentle end to the day ∎

ROUTE 2: BETHESDA TO THE CARNEDDAU

A long and memorable walk that lends itself to several variations. A dull start into a mountain valley leads to increasingly dramatic and rugged scenery culminating in Carnedd Dafydd (1044m). The high and easy ridge to Carnedd Llywelyn (1064m) reveals a wide panorama of hills and valleys. The return offers an exhilarating walk giving excellent near views but alas ends in a moorland slog.

Know Before You Go In poor conditions take navigational care on the summit of Carnedd Llywelyn. In all conditions take navigational care as you approach enclosed land towards the end of the route. Parking is limited at Gerlan.

Getting There The ideal starting point is in Gerlan (gr 6366), well uphill from Bethesda but parking is severely restricted there. So if you have one or few cars, park in Gerlan by turning left off the A5 (coming from Bangor) just before the Spar supermarket, fork right almost immediately, continue straight on uphill to park anywhere on or around Fford Gerlan. Otherwise park in one of several free car parks in the village of Bethesda. **Bus**: Bethesda (especially) and Gerlan are well served from Bangor or even Caernarfon.

Walking Time 5.25 hours from Gerlan (distance 14km, climb 1060m).

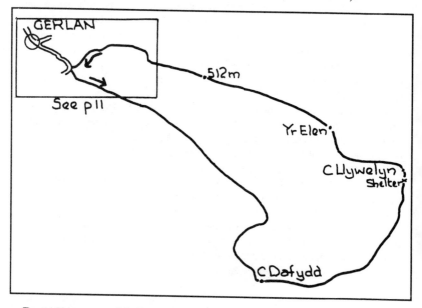

Route If you started in Bethesda (gr 6266) walk up to Fford Gerlan (see under Getting There above) and with the disused post office on the left head south-east out of the village along a narrow road. Cross two bridges and just after the second take a right of way on the left heading south-east through rough farmland. The path is not very distinct in places but if you continue resolutely south-east you will gradually leave dullish upland country and enter much wilder mountain land with Afon Llafar off to the left.

If you have doubts about navigation you can follow the long rising spur of short grass on the right, Mynydd Du, which takes you with only one small drop towards the summit of Carnedd Dafydd. The long views on this spur are excellent but why not try a more subtle route? To do this continue up the valley on an initially good path, but where it fades (at about gr 665639) in a deep rocky pocket with an imposing cliff ahead, climb steeply west uphill following a narrow stream. This will allow you to emerge far up Mynydd Du with a small top just to the right. Turn south-east uphill here to shortly reach a difficult boulder field guarding the approach to the summit of Carnedd Dafydd. Here keep to the right away from the cliff to reach an intermittent path that is marginally better than the bouldery alternative.

Carnedd Dafydd (1044m) commands views to the sharply pointed Elidir Fawr to the west, over the Snowdonia massif to the south-west and south, the Glyderau close at hand to the south and a whole array of lesser mountains (where not blocked by its taller brother, Llywelyn to the north-east) in other directions.

Now for Llywelyn. Follow the gentle curve of high ground around the valley of the Afon Llafar east and eventually north, evading or climbing a few areas of boulders. Llywelyn (1064m) is not a place to be on a bad day since there is an extensive summit plateau of short grass and stones with the route you want not exactly obvious. If you take a bearing of 320° from the **first shelter** you meet you should reach an outcrop on the far end of the plateau

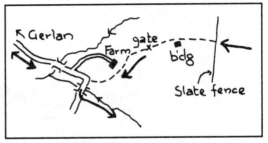

and from there pick up a path heading about west towards Yr Elen (962m) mostly on a narrow ridge, passing the cliffs overlooking brooding Cwm Caseg – a memorable sight – and then climbing a short distance to the summit. On the map the descent from Yr Elen looks a little hazardous but in fact there is a steep but easy zig-zag path north-west.

You might note that after Yr Elen there are three small but distinct rocky outcrops on your way west into progressively duller moorland. After the third, point 512m at gr 6565, continue roughly west into an area of deep rushes, watching out as you go for a slate fence across your path; cross it at a point where there is a gate and waymark to pass a **disused building**. Cross the gate straight ahead just beyond it and then follow the yellow on black arrows (you may have to look carefully around for them) to walk to the left of a farmhouse and thus gain the road. Walk down to Gerlan ∎

ROUTE 3: CREIGIAU GLEISION

A short, memorable route though with some difficult navigation and underfoot conditions. The central section high above and beyond the shores of Llyn Cowlyd Reservoir is a series of exhilarating rocky hummocks giving excellent views.

Know Before You Go The second half of the upland section of the route is quite difficult navigationally, with occasional nasty but avoidable crags and intermittent or misleading paths.

Getting There Drive to Trefriw (gr 7863) on the B5106. Here take the road on the right (if headed towards Betws-y-coed) signposted Llyn Grafnant. It's initially very steep; for its entire length of less than 2 miles it's narrow. An alternative starting point at Capel Curig is given below.

Walking Time The distance is 13km, and the climb 730m if you climb every last hillock on the second half of the southward leg. This, in theory should take 4.5 hours, but with the steep and tortuous descents and navigational difficulties could easily take an hour more. If you skip these hillocks it will reduce the climb by only about 70m but the time should be much nearer the theoretical.

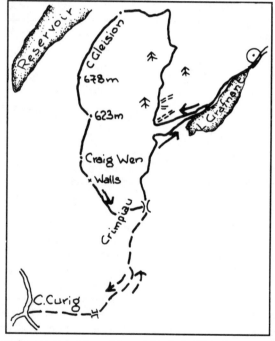

Route From the car park (charge) turn right, fork right when you reach the lake and, now on a track, walk along the lake into forest. Fork first right uphill in the forest, walk round a hairpin bend and immediately take a path on the left heading steeply uphill. From here on the general rule is to head north and uphill, with only a few metres on track and the rest on minimally waymarked path. The last section of path ends at a forest edge after an extremely wet, mostly contouring, section, where you will probably be glad to hear that it is open country from here on.

Follow fence posts through high heather to a crossways fence high on the north-east shoulder of Creigiau Gleision and, with views opening up in all directions, here turn left to follow a better fence steeply upwards. Leave the fence at its highest point to face the rocky ground to the south-west.

What follows for the next two kilometres is a delightful walk: excellent views especially on the right down to Llyn Cowlyd Reservoir and the Carneddau, the Glyderau nearly ahead, a moderately good path underfoot and easy navigation.

First climb to the northern summit of Creigiau Gleision (634m), after which is a striking band of white quartzite. Continue along the rocky plateau to the highest point of the day, the substantial cairn on summit 678m. From here your route bends subtly left to cross a boggy area and a minor top at gr 730609.

From here on we are into navigational difficulties. The basic idea is simple: to reach the bwlch at gr 739597. The problem is that you might be tempted to climb several craggy tops that have non-negotiable (to me anyway) slabs on their descent (and therefore harder) side: if you do climb them be prepared for some backtracking. You can avoid the tops altogether by keeping them nearby on your left, but this route is less scenic. In either case you will have to cross a few soggy flat plains between the hillocks – quite a contrast to the tops.

Good news! After Craig Wen (548m) you will encounter a **network of walls** (gr 729599), a great help in navigation. Keep the wall that heads roughly south-east on the right until it turns decisively left and descends steeply towards the valley of Llyn Grafnant. You might venture to climb the next grassy hillock, Crimpiau (475m), after which you should be able to cautiously pick your way the few hundred metres to the bwlch and clear path coming up from Capel Curig.

When you reach this path you might wish to dispense with the next paragraph's boringly detailed description. Here it is anyway as briefly as possible.

Turn left onto the path to pass through a narrow gap and head down towards Llyn Grafnant. When, near the valley floor, you reach a high wall, turn right to cross the first stile over it. Beyond it take a path directly to a nearby house and pick up the track at it. Shortly fork left onto a grassy path, and at its nearby end turn left onto another track that passes in front of the house Tan-y-Manod. Just beyond it turn right over a bridge and follow the yellow-tipped markers to a forest track. Turn right here and as you are now surely sick of detailed directions you will be glad to hear that it is straight on to the start.

Capel Curig Start The total distance is 15km and the climb 900m so in theory the walking time is 5.25 hours but the strictures given above apply equally to this variation..

A pleasant and easy approach, even if you will have to do it twice. Take the right of way opposite the shops at the junction of the A5 and the A4086 and just to the left of the church. Keep on it over a bridge seemingly designed to deter those who would throw themselves river-ward, turn left here into increasingly stern and craggy mountain land with a miasmic swamp close on the left at one point to reach the bwlch. You can then follow the commentary at the last paragraph of the main route above, but forking acutely first left in forest and picking up the commentary again near its start. ∎

ROUTE 4: ABER FALLS TO GARNEDD UCHAF

A stiff climb close to the popular Aber Waterfall ends in a soggy plateau punctuated by unexpected bouldery mounds as far as Garnedd Uchaf, after which is a high-level walk to Drum. From here on the terrain is dull and gently sloped but with wide seaward views. A satisfying but not over-exciting circuit.

Know Before You Go There are some navigationally problematic areas of featureless bogland but it is generally possible to cut your losses and head valley-ward, with Llyn Anafon being a good target if you wish to forego the duller last third of the walk.

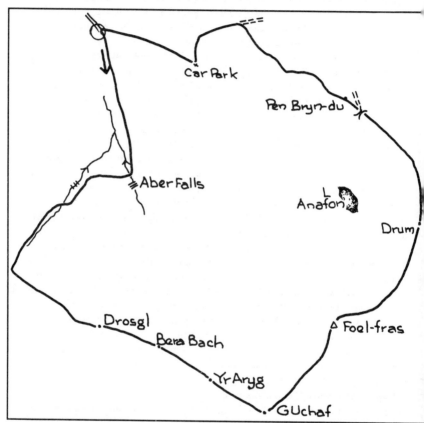

Getting There Come off the A55 at exit 13 to drive through the village of Abergwyngregyn. Here follow the signs for Aber Falls for less than a mile to a car park on the right just before a bridge (gr 662720) (charge). Alternatively you can also drive on to an informal car park at the road's end (gr 676715, no charge) and start the walk from there. **Bus:** there is a frequent service (5, X5) to Abergwyngregyn.

Walking Time 6.5 hours (distance 18km, climb 1100m) but leave some time to explore the bouldery castles at Bera Bach and perhaps Bera Mawr.

Route Follow the track south to Aber Falls, emulate the admiring crowds by gawking at it and turn west on a path to cross a bridge just below another waterfall. At the second waterfall past Aber, cross a stile on the left and prepare for a steep climb along the tumbling Afon Gam.

This is rough country and since the left bank (true) is the easier farther up, cross the stream where you can and climb steeply along the side of its impressive gorge until it peters out quite suddenly in wet uplands. From here head south-east to Drosgl, maybe picking up a path on the way that is slightly better than nothing.

Drosgyl (758m) is a modest peak of cairns on a rock-strewn area; farther on to the east, and much more dramatic, are Bera Mawr (794m) and Bera Bach (807m), mighty castles of rocks and a startling sight in this otherwise nondescript landscape. You could profitably spend some time clambering over these castles but only Bera Bach, the one to the right, is on the route and you can evade it should you wish.

The next target is Yr Arug to the south-east, a much more modest affair of shards of boulders. From here to the next summit, Garnedd Uchaf, you should be able to see the northern end of the Glyderau to the south-west with Yr Elen and Carnedd Llywelyn nearby and roughly south. Garnedd Uchaf (926m), the highest point on the route, is similar to Yr Arug and even less inclined than it to rise above the general level hereabouts. However from here a clear path heads north-east to the next summit, Foel-fras, reached over a particularly scenic stretch.

Foel-fras (842m) has a **trig pillar** so you cannot mistake it. Unfortunately from here on the underfoot conditions are dull; to compensate the views seaward excellent. At least the navigation is easy: follow a fence downhill, initially east, but bending left to reach Drum (770m), which has a shelter but nothing much else to recommend it.

From Drum take a track north for about two kilometres to a shallow bwlch. You can take this track to tarmac but it is worthwhile leaving it here and heading over the bumpy, heathery spur to Pen Bryn-du and beyond because of the excellent views it gives leftward into the valley of the Afon Anafon.

One could expend many words explaining how to get to the informal car park at gr 676715 but all you really need to know is that you have to reach a track running east-west on the near side of two sets of extremely high voltage pylons; to do so keep roughly to the crest of the spur as far as Foel-ganol (533m) and then continue roughly north-west, bearing right if steep ground threatens. When you reach the track turn left for tarmac and the car park; then take the steep road beyond it down to the start ■

Note

Bogland. The area covered by this route is one of the most noted (or notorious) in Snowdonia for its thick covering of peat, most of it blanketing the terrain above about 800m. Analysis of pollen taken from the peat indicates seed of birch, alder and hazel, which today do not grow much above 250m. These trees must have flourished about 8000 years ago when the climate was comparatively warm and dry.

ROUTE 5: PEN YR HELGI DU AND PEN LLITHRIG Y WRACH

Not the most inspiring route in the Carneddau but one offering excellent long distance views; good for summer weekends since you are likely to have much of the area to yourself. After an excruciating slog up a concrete road a stiff climb ends at a memorable bwlch. From here the two lofty peaks (833m and 799m) with the impressive monikers given in the title above can be tackled. The walk ends by traversing soggy moorland.

Know Before You Go There's some wet ground and one easy scramble. Parts are a little difficult navigationally but this is an area without many cliffs so an escape route or shorter variation is generally possible.

Getting There If you are in a large party park in the campsite at Gwern Gof Isaf (gr 6860) (small charge) on the A5 over 2 miles from either Idwal Cottage or Capel Curig. If you have only one or two cars you could chance parking at the entrance to the side road a little farther east at gr 687603, but do not block the road. **Bus:** S6 from Bethesda or Betws-y-coed.

Walking Time 3.75 hours (distance 10km, climb 700m).

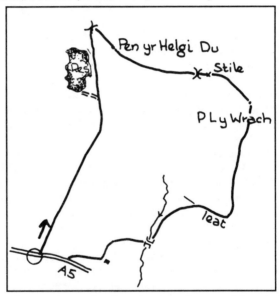

Route Assuming you are starting from the camp site, turn right out of it, walk a few metres and then turn left onto an ugly tarmac, straight road. Slog for over 2km uphill and where it turns sharply left and downhill leave the road at about a ruin on the right to pass to the right of the large Ffynnon Llugwy Reservoir. Here pick up a clear path heading directly up to the bwlch between Carnedd Llywelyn on the left and Pen yr Helgi Du on the right. This bwlch has abrupt climbs to north-west and south-east and equally abrupt falls at right angles to these (you will know all about the climb from the Reservoir). The view down into the depths of Cwm Eigiau is particularly impressive.

Onwards and upwards. Turn right (south-east) for the climb to Pen yr Helgi Du. To do this take the clear but gulp-inducingly steep path initially to the right of the crest and later on it, buoyed up, I trust, in the knowledge that the start of the climb is the most difficult. The summit of Pen yr Helgi Du (833m) is most unimpressive and indicated only by an IKEA flat-pack set of rocks that have not yet been assembled into a proper cairn; but the views are excellent, with the Glyderau and in particular Tryfan to south and south-west.

Pass two inexplicably placed cairns on the short grass just off the summit and continue to the next bwlch, the one facing Pen Llitrig y Wrach, a scenic but much more modest affair than the last one but with a **stile** at gr 709628, possibly a useful landmark in really bad conditions.

The climb to Pen Llithrig y Wrach (799m) is straightforward: simply keep to the crest on a clear path heading east and swing right for the modest summit cairn. The views, from here encompassing Llyn Cowlyd Reservoir along with variations of those seen from Pen yr Helgi Du, are most impressive. On the descent initially keep this Reservoir in view on the left; later, by keeping to the vague crest of the spur south from the summit, you will traverse a rough, boggy (where not craggy) terrain running all the way down to the A5.

Long before the A5 however you will cross a stile ahead and turn right at a leat (a contouring water channel) beyond it. Follow the leat to the second bridge along and here descend diagonally through dispiriting moorland following a wide but soggy path.

Curiously the path disappears as it reaches a river, the Afon y Bedol, leaving you to squelch downhill along it and cross on a slab bridge just above enclosed fields. Take the waymarked path beyond the bridge initially uphill following a wall and turn left onto a track after about 500m (this turn is waymarked but you will have to watch out for it). This track takes you eventually to the A5 with the start a few hundred metres along to the right ■

ROUTE 6: CWM EIGIAU AND CARNEDD LLYWELYN

A gentle stroll into the deep recesses of the long, brooding valley of remote Cwm Eigiau is followed by an exciting but avoidable steep and pathless ascent to a bwlch in the high Carneddau, beyond which is Carnedd Llywelyn (1044m). The descent is through another upland valley.

Know Before You Go There is a lot of pathless ground and consequently fairly difficult navigation in places. Please minimise the number of cars you take (see below).

Getting There There's more than enough excitement in even getting to the start of this walk, what with an extremely steep and winding narrow gated road and the distinct possibility of not so mobile impediments in the form of cows and sheep to contend with. The details: from Conwy take the B5106 and turn right just after the public house Y Bedol (the road is unsigned) in the village of Tal-y-Bont (gr 7668). Drive onward for 3 miles to the car park.

Walking Time 4.75 hours (distance 14km, climb 700m).

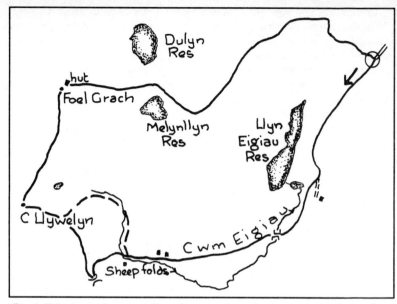

Route Take the track onward from the car park south-west across bleak moorland passing by the giant walls of the breached dam that once spanned Llyn Eigiau Reservoir. Walk parallel to these walls, so crossing over the main stream in the valley. Just beyond it fork right over a plank bridge before a house surrounded by trees. Continue on the track back over the river and farther on along a rising track penetrating deep into Cwm Eigiau, here penned in by towering Pen y Helgi Du and Pen Llithrig y Wrach straight ahead and on the left respectively and by gently-sloped moorland on the right.

At length the track comes in effect to an end at two sets of long abandoned mine buildings, with the main stream in the valley close by them. Continue up the valley from these buildings for a short distance until the stream swings sharply left in its direction of travel and here watch out for **two tiny sheep folds** on the opposite bank. About here you will have to make a decision.

You may like to ascend to the high bwlch to the south-west – possibly a less than enticing prospect. The advantage of this approach is that it gives you a more memorable route, though you may like to forego that if you think you might end up in hospital, which would make the day memorable but not in an enjoyable way. However it can be done: in fact I did it only on one foot (the other being in the grave). The line of ascent is between a minor crag on the left and a mighty one on the right but there is no useful path until you get high up, so you may have to pull yourself up by clinging onto heather bushes. When the path finally appears it runs diagonally from right to left.

When you do get to the bwlch, a magnificent viewpoint, turn right, climb the steep rocky slope ahead and take the rising path all the way to Carnedd Llywelyn to the north-west.

Now suppose you eschew this approach. Continue up Cwm Eigiau keeping close to the main stream and when you reach a major tributary keep to the left (more west) branch, that's the one that has cut a deep cleft in the steep ground above. Beyond the cleft follow the stream for another few hundred metres and here look out for a suitable place to the south-west to ascend to the crest of the ridge – there's a fair choice. Turn right at the crest on a clear path for Carnedd Llywelyn's summit plateau.

From Carnedd Llywelyn (1064m) take navigational care: you have to descend the rocky ridge north towards Foel Grach and from Llywelyn's extensive plateau it's not all that simple. One hint: keep steep ground on the right all the way up Carnedd Llywelyn and some of the way down. However a compass bearing might be a good idea in any conditions. Once you get some way down the slope towards Foel Grach take the wide path heading for this summit and climb it. On the other side you should come across an **emergency hut**, a sure indication of your position no matter how bad the weather. From this hut head initially east between the lakes of Dulyn and Melynllyn, each set in a magnificent cliff-bound corrie gouged high in otherwise none too exciting moorland. There is no clear path down but the underfoot conditions are easy with only the occasional rocky outcrop and soggy area to avoid.

When you reach the end of a track on the northern end of Melynllyn you might be happy to know that you simply cannot go wrong. Take the track all the way back to the start; it gives excellent views down into the valley of Afon Dulyn with its occasional copse of trees and abandoned house. A relaxing ending to what was hopefully a not too demanding day ■

Note

Cwm Eigiau. A valley with a tragic history. From where you are at this bwlch you are looking down into the upper valley, which curves left until it loses itself in flatter country a few kilometres down. It holds a large reservoir, Llyn Eigiau and as you will see if you walk Route 6, the reservoir dam has been breached. The lake was used to hold water for a hydro-electric scheme and was commissioned in 1908. Unfortunately during heavy rain in 1925, the dam burst and a flood of water, stones and mud swept down the valley all the way to the village of Dolgarrog about 5km away. Sixteen people were killed and the numbers would have been higher had so many people not been in the village cinema.

THE GLYDERAU

ROUTE 7: TRYFAN BY THE HEATHER TERRACE

You cannot mistake Tryfan (915m). Rearing abruptly like a giant stone armadillo south of the A5 it stands aloof from the main Glyderau range. Only ibexes will find it easy to make the climb through the boulders guarding the summit; in addition this route takes a challenging route across the mountain's eastern slopes. A memorable day in store!

Know Before You Go Avoid this route if the rocks are likely to be wet. This route gets to the summit via the navigationally difficult but exhilarating Heather Terrace. You can avoid the Terrace by taking the variation of Route 8.

Getting There The start is on the A5 just to the east of Llyn Ogwen (about gr 668605). Coming from Bethesda pass Llyn Ogwen and park just beyond it on a straight stretch of road offering plenty of parking. From Capel Curig park around the dense copse of trees on the right just before Llyn Ogwen about 4 miles from Capel Curig. **Bus**: S6 from Bethesda or Betws-y-coed.

Walking Time The time to the summit of Tryfan is infinitely variable, depending as it does on your ability, on how wet the rocks are and on (not quite providentially) hitting the right path - of which more anon. The walking time (in theory) is a mere 2.25 hours (distance 5km, climb 620m) but reckon on half that again.

Route Cross the stile directly opposite the dense copse and the gate on the right just beyond it. From here, with a myriad of beckoning paths going every which way you might as well ignore them all and head roughly south and upward keeping the flank of Tryfan to the right and the mighty slabs of Little Tryfan, usually festooned with acolyte climbers, off to the left.

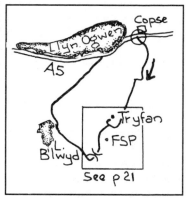

When you see a crossways fence ahead, do not cross it. Instead follow a clear path rightward and upward into a narrow gully (gr 667599), climb it and prepare for trouble.

A word about the Heather Terrace, the 'path' traversing this face of Tryfan. It is easily observable from a distance but perversely quite difficult to find when you are at it; this applies particularly to the first section that you are now about to tackle. If all else fails remember that if you lose it a bearing of 200° will keep you roughly in the right direction and you have a good chance (but no more than that) of picking it up again. Lastly remember that not all paths around here are the Heather Terrace: there are other paths heading I know not where.

Off we go! Turn left at the top of the gully, cross a scree slope and, while clambering over rocks, keep looking out for traces of a path heading roughly in the right direction. Eventually, the path, running between fearsome crags to right (up) and left (down), becomes a lot clearer, though it still requires the occasional clamber.

At length, and here the path is easy to follow, you will see a path heading up over slabs to the right. Do not take it: instead continue on for a few more metres, now gently downhill, until you reach an eroded scree slope; scramble up it to the crest of the spur above and cross the wall (it's only about 100m long) at the stile on the right to face the final assault.

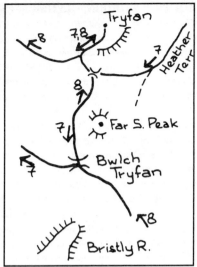

From this stile walk away from the wall round the base of the awe-inspiring cliffs close at hand, so heading moderately down, until after about 30 double steps you see disturbed rocks and scrape marks indicating a path of sorts heading north-east and upward. This is the route you want, but before you start up try to remember it as this is the way you will return.

The path is fine for a while but then in fades in mighty boulders as it swings left (north). Just before the summit, cross a bridge of boulders and then . . . congratulations! You are there on the tiny summit, with the two proud rocks, Adam and Eve, to keep you company, along with the heroes and heroines who have come up the life-threatening northern face. And by the way, tradition has it that you should jump from Adam to Eve, though if you fear that you may soon after encounter another A and E it might not be prudent to try it.

Return by the same route to the wall and then negotiate your way round and down the right side of Far South Peak until you come to the deep Bwlch Tryfan, traversed by about 400m of wall and four stiles strung between Far South Peak and the menacing Bristly Ridge. Take the clear path from the farthest stile north-west to Llyn Bochlwyd, cross the outlet stream and take the made path down steep ground. Where the slope eases cross the stream and head back roughly north-east to either of the car parks on the non-lake side of Llyn Ogwen, hopefully picking up a path on the way. From the car park turn right onto the road and walk to the start ■

ROUTE 8: Y GRIBIN, GLYDER FACH AND TRYFAN

The walk with two difficult climbs – the steep and fairly hazardous Y Gribin and the bouldery but comparatively level ascent to Tryfan, though the latter can be bypassed. Between, the exhilarating splendours of the high Glyderau.

Know Before You Go Though hard to be objective about it, the scramble up Y Gribin is not all that difficult if you take time to ensure that you are on a viable route: this may involve some anxious moments. Consolation: it will be much easier the second time. Unfortunately a retreat from Y Gribin means resorting to the variation, a much less satisfying route.

Getting There Park in the first off-road car park (gr 656602) on the landward side past Idwal Cottage. If you have to park elsewhere start the walk by climbing diagonally up towards the one and only major stream debouching into Llyn Ogwen. **Bus:** S6 from Bethesda or Betws-y-coed.

Walking Time 3.5 hours (distance 7km, climb 750m) including 0.5 hours extra for scrambling up Y Gribin and on the difficult terrain of the Glyderau.

Route Take the well-marked path south, which unfortunately comes to an indeterminate end near a swiftly flowing stream on the right. Cross it anywhere and continue up through rough ground to reach a made path ascending beside the upper rapids of this stream, the outlet from Llyn Bochlwyd. Keep on this path to the plateau holding the lake.

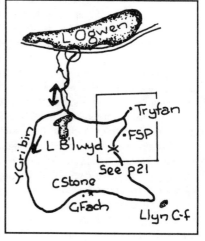

Llyn Bochlwyd is tucked into a dramatic mountain location, with Tryfan and the Bristly Ridge to east and south-east and, close to west and south-west, the rocky spur of Y Gribin, the next and crucial climb. So with the lake initially close on the left walk to the foot of Y Gribin and take a clear path rising steadily to a tiny plateau beyond which rears the hardest part of the day's walk.

It's difficult to describe in detail exactly how to climb this formidable spur. You can keep to the crest and face a few anxious moments of vertigo (probably the better option) or stay on the right of the crest and look out for any snatches of path, scrapes in the rock, or newly disturbed boulders to help you. Easiest of all, you can ignominiously follow someone else or wait for someone coming behind to help you. However it could turn out that the competent looking chap you are waiting for is hoping that you can pioneer the route!

Eventually you will be able to attain the crest of the spur and make your way through boulders to a shelter poised on the edge of the Glyderau plateau. You're there, specifically at Bwlch y Ddwy-Glyder with Castell y Gwynt, the mighty heaps of rock strewn at all angles close at hand to the south-east.

From here on the navigational rule is to head roughly east. First keep Castell y Gwynt on the left and a little farther on Glyder Fach (994m) on the right. Just beyond the latter is the unmissable **Cantilever Stone** (gr 657583), a useful landmark. The views along here are magnificent, particularly towards nearby Tryfan.

Beyond the Cantilever Stone descend through rocks, slightly aided by the occasional cairn, until you are within 200m or so of Llyn Caseg-fraith, the only major lake around. Here look out for a path heading *diagonally* down and to the left (north-west). Take it until, after a steep descent of ten minutes or so (it's hard to be precise) you pass close by a few tiny lakes. Time to head up to Bwlch Tryfan, the low point on the horizon to the north-west, taking a(ny) rough path.

There is a wall at the Bwlch that is about 400m long and is crossed by four stiles (see the inset sketch map on page 21). The Bwlch terminates on the south part-way up the rocky lower reaches of the dreaded Bristly Ridge and on the north by the impenetrable crags of, not Tryfan, but Tryfan's Far South Peak. So now, unlike me on my first foray, you will not attempt to climb these crags in the mistaken idea that you are climbing Tryfan.

Cross the wall at the south of the Bwlch. From here you can head straight down to Llyn Bochlwyd and home on a good path but if you are Tryfan-bound head north and climb on one of any number of virtually useless paths, keeping the summit of Far South Peak on the right, until you reach a section of wall about 100m long with two stiles bridging a narrow bwlch. The summit of Tryfan is now directly to the north but, from here, don't try a direct approach unless you are an aficionado of ropeless rock climbing. Instead follow the suggestions of Route 7.

Safely back at the foot of the steep bouldery ground aim down initially at 290° through scree and rough ground. Farther down pick up a path heading down to near the northern end of Llyn Bochlwyd, and cross the outlet stream on nature-bestowed stepping stones. Take your upward route down, making sure not to follow the made path indefinitely. Instead cross over the stream when you get to less steep ground and head north for the car park ■

VARIATION: TRYFAN THE REALLY EASY WAY

This variation is nearly a straight up and down. Nonetheless it is an enjoyable route and gives you some insight into the harsh terrain around Tryfan and towards the Glyderau with minimum effort and navigational difficulties.

Know Before You Go Take care over the boulders of the last 70m climb to Tryfan's summit.

Getting There As above.

Walking Time 2 hours (distance 4km, climb 620m) in theory but allow longer.

Route In brief. Take the main route to Llyn Bochlwyd; here follow the clear path south-east to Bwlch Tryfan; then resume the description under the main route as given in the last two paragraphs above (see also the inset sketch map on page 21) ■

ROUTE 9: THE NORTHERN GLYDERAU

The northern end of the Glyderau falls in rugged cliffs and steep grassy slopes to the A5. This scenically magnificent route traverses the high ground above these from Bethesda to Idwal Cottage (gr 6460) and culminates in Y Garn (947m). This is an A to B route so you will have to take the bus back or walk 8km on the cycleway at the end.

Know Before You Go Unless you have compelling reasons otherwise do this route in the direction suggested. This is because if you walk south to north it could be quite difficult to get off the high ground at the correct point and, if you wander too far north, you will reach very hostile terrain above the slate quarry at Bethesda. Note also that the ground above Cwm Ceunant is rough; that there are few easy escape routes and that navigation is generally simple.

Getting There Just south of Bethesda there is limited parking on the B4409 close to the bridge at its junction with the A5 (gr 624659). Don't park on the section of road owned by the slate company. **Bus**: Bethesda is well served and there is a good service on the S6 back from Idwal Cottage.

Walking Time 4 hours (distance 10km, climb 980m) as an A to B walk. Allow 1.75 hours for the walk back to the start.

Route Assuming you park at the bridge take the road south with the swirling Afon Ogwen leaping over slabs way down in the wooded valley to the left. After a few minutes take the gate on the left to continue along the wide cycleway past a huge mound of slate.

Past the slate you will come to the first gate on the right at a point with a house, the first, less than 500m ahead. This gate leads into the indistinct Cwm Ceunant. Follow the stream uphill on either bank, but remember that you are eventually going to pick up a clear path on the right of the stream. This wayward path heads first helpfully parallel to the stream, then diverts away from it, then resumes its upward route and finally loses all interest in the proceedings and peters out in low heather and bilberries.

This is where the going, underfoot and navigationally, is a little fraught. Head diagonally right uphill until you reach the crest of the spur where, providentially there is a clear path reaching to the northern top of Carnedd Filiast (721m), and you can relax with the knowledge that from here on, in good conditions anyway, most of the next 4km will be delightful, with great views over the rugged cliffs to the left plunging way down into Nant Ffrancon.

From the northern top head south, a little down and a little more up to the southern summit (821m), guarded by a boulder field, over which you will have to hop or teeter your way (keeping to the left may be easier). Continue south-east over a **high wall** at about gr 622626, a good landmark in bad weather. Then keep the cliffs close on the left over easy ground with minor boulder fields, noting at one point how the cliff edge swings abruptly from east to south. Follow the cliff all the way to the almost non-existent summit of Mynydd Perfedd (812m) – the shelter on the short grass plain is the best indicator of its position.

From here only a genius could get lost. From Mynydd Perfedd descend south-east (not south-west towards Elidir Fawr) on a path to Bwlch Brecan and then divert left from the main path onto a steep, winding stony one to the summit of Foel-goch (831m), another excellent viewing point. Then continue downhill and south to a narrow bwlch before resuming the climb through shattered stones and pebbles to the highest point of the day, Y Garn (947m). On the way there it would be prudent to note your clear descent path on the left, marked by a cairn (*unfortunately one of several hereabouts*).

Y Garn is a magnificent viewpoint: the Carneddau to the north-east, the rugged cliffs on the eastern and northern side of the Glyderau at your feet, the highly distinctive hump of Tryfan close by to the east, and the Snowdon massif to the south.

Retrace your steps to the path noted on the ascent. It leads east steeply down on a narrow spur, giving predictably excellent views over a great complex of cliffs and cwms around large Llyn Idwal before eventually landing you near the shores of the lake itself.

From here you can take the prominent path initially running north-east from the *north-east* corner of the lake back to Idwal Cottage but it is more interesting to head north-east from its *northern* end along what initially seems to be an invisible right of way. This starting point will allow you to pick up a path through a narrow gorge with rocky vertical sides, an unusual phenomenon hereabouts, and then back to the A5 and the bus.

If you have to walk back to Bethesda you have nearly 8km on a cycleway parallel, but not too close to, the road. A pleasant walk, if a little tame after what has gone before ■

ROUTE 10: THE GLYDERAU FROM NANT PERIS TO PEN-Y-PASS.

The central 4km-long section of the Glyderau is a most memorable walk, attracting many – too many? – walkers. A plateau, much of it over 950m, it commands excellent views over cwms and cliffs and reveals varied angles on the incomparable Tryfan. Boulder fields and immense piles of rocks strewn across the plateau make for difficult walking. Before this is a steep but scenic climb and after it a dullish end. Nonetheless a walk not to be missed.

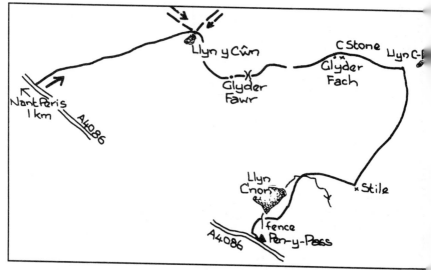

Know Before You Go The rocky ground – dangerously slippery when wet – over much of the route has already been alluded to. In poor visibility it is difficult to navigate over the plateau because of mounds of rocks; a dogged progress roughly east until you are out of this country just beyond the one distinct landmark, the Cantilever Rock, might be the best bet. This is an A to B walk so you will have to return on the frequent S1 bus from Pen-y-Pass. Alternatively you might prefer the looped variation (below) from Idwal Cottage.

Getting There Start in the village of Nant Peris (gr 6058) where there is a free car park (by bus you could asked to be dropped at the next stop). There is a good bus service from Bangor and Caernarfon to Llanberis and thence on the S1 bus along the A4086.

Walking Time 5.25 hours (distance 11km, climb 980m) including 45 minutes more than Naismith on the plateau and 15 minutes for the swampy cross-country route at the end, should you choose it.

Route Turn right from the car park to walk about 1km (seems more) along the unyielding A4086. Here turn left at the bus stop sign and footpath post. Follow the path upward and east, so crossing a major tributary of the Afon Las on a metal bridge. Continue upward on a rocky, steep path – an excellent stretch to admire the view behind of the slowly revealed valley of the Pass of Llanberis. This path takes you directly to a broad bwlch with Tryfan peeping over the near horizon. Walk to the far end of the large Llyn y Cŵn and mentally prepare for the climb to the Glyderau plateau.

Starting from the north end of the lake pick your way south on a steep, intermittent path through patches of scree and between crags to a clearer but unpleasant gravelly path farther up. This ascends to level ground on the plateau, and to the great heap of rocks constituting Glyder Fawr (999m), which you may like to climb if you don't mind risking a broken ankle.

From Glyder Fawr continue down to a shallow but distinct bwlch (957m) and then make a slight detour, a climb north-east over short grass to a shelter giving great views north. From here descend slightly to the vague Bwlch y Ddwy-Glyder and then keep to the right of the great heap of boulders ahead, which is Castell y Gwynt, and to the left of the next heap, Glyder Fach (994m). Just beyond it is the unmistakeable **Cantilever Stone** (gr 657583), the only sure landmark in this area, and a little farther on the end of the Bristly Ridge with Tryfan beyond it.

From the junction with the Bristly Ridge, though it is still bouldery underfoot, it is easier to navigate in a quasi-straight line. Descend east on a fairly clear path and when you are within 300m or so of **Llyn Caseg-fraith** (it's a lake), turn right (south) along the Miner's Path over boggy ground initially, but on a distinct path once past the first rocky outcrop.

A hard choice when you reach a **stile** at the corner of a wall. You can continue on the path down to Pen-y-Gwryd and then slog for 20 minutes up the A4086. Alternatively, you can take the adventurous, obstacle-strewn approach by heading across boggy country and around rocky slabs, which has the snag that you are sure to see the bus pulling out dead on time just as you reach Pen-y-Pass.

Let's consider the adventurous option. Head west from the stile to cross the outlet stream from Llyn Cwmffynnon a few hundred metres from the lake and on the stream's far bank cross a stile at a fence junction. Then head south keeping the lake a hundred metres or more off to the right to avoid slabs nearer it. Near the south end of the lake follow another fence south and cross at the first stile. Walk 100m or so west and then due south and down; this will take you, crags close on the left, to a gate close to the youth hostel. Shake your fist at the departing bus!

Long Variation: Climb the spur starting in gr 6159 as described in Route 12 and then Foel-goch (you can avoid but it offers excellent views) and Y Garn before joining the main route around Llyn y Cŵn. This (including Foel-goch) makes a total walking time of 6 hours (distance 15km, climb 1200m) including one hour over Naismith for the reasons given above.

Variation from the North: This is the same route as the above on the Glyderau ridge but you won't need the bus. Park at the car park at Idwal Cottage (charge). It is then a navigationally easy walk to Llyn Idwal (follow the crowds) and up the made path south via the initially fearsome looking Devil's Kitchen to near Llyn y Cŵn. Follow the main route above to within 300m of **Llyn Caseg-fraith** and here follow Route 8 to Bwlch Tryfan and thence down to Llyn Bochlwyd. There is a path from here north-west to the start. Walking time 4.25 hours (distance 8km, climb 840m) allowing 45 minutes over Naismith as above ∎

ROUTE 11: CAPEL CURIG TO THE EASTERN GLYDERAU

A suitable route for a day of low cloud since much of it is in the lower mountains, even if the highest point is over 800m. A long, gradual climb over undulating mountain country ends in lofty Y Foel Goch. The return is along the rocky northern spur of this mountain and finishes with an easy stroll on the valley floor.

Know Before You Go Few difficulties apart from negotiating the rock wall after Y Foel Goch. This route may be easily done in reverse, thus leaving the valley walk for the start, should the day look as if it going to clear up later (see below).

Getting There Park in the free car park just off the junction of the A5 and the A4086 in Capel Curig. **Bus:** S6 from Bethesda. S2 and S6 from Betws-y-coed.

Walking Time 4 hours (distance 12km, climb 680m).

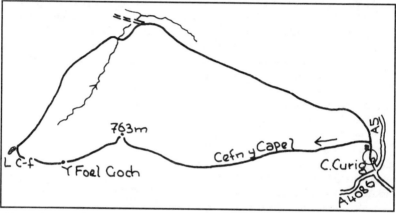

Route Turn right out of the car park and walk a few metres beyond the first farmhouse on the left. Here turn left up a path and follow it resolutely upward and westward through a terrain of ribs of exposed rock, the path's exact direction not helped by indistinct stretches and sub-paths that have fundamental differences of opinion as to their exact goal.

At length the path becomes clearer and the terrain easier. Still heading west, you will find yourself on the left of an indeterminate crest, rising to the nondescript Cefn y Capel (460m) and then sinking into soggy bogland before the distinct and moderately tough climb to the unnamed summit 763m. On this climb the rocky spur of Gallt yr Ogof falling north towards the main valley is the focus. It's worthwhile diverging right from the path to reach this summit, or rather two cairned summits about 100m apart, between which is a rocky plateau.

Rejoining the path the next summit is Y Foel Goch (805m), the highest point of the route. It is furnished with a shelter and cairn and offers great views, with the Snowdon massif to the south-west and the Carneddau to the north being particularly notable.

From Y Foel Goch take the path west and down for a few minutes to a flat, soggy area where a few minor lakes lurk in anonymous and well-deserved obscurity, beyond which is the much larger but no more distinguished Llyn Caseg-fraith. From it head down the rocky spur of Braich y Ddeugwm to the north-east taking care to avoid crags in its upper reaches. Along here there are majestic views to Tryfan with the Heather Terrace prominent across its nearby face. Would that it were equally prominent when you are trying to find your way up it!

As you descend you will note that the spur you are on divides into two sub-spurs, a grassy one to the left, a rockier one to the right. To maintain the views of Tryfan you might like to keep to the leftward, this involving a very short rise.

Nearing the valley floor of the A5 remember that at some point you will have to cross the main stream, Nant yr Ogof, in the valley on your right. One way of doing this is to climb a stile in a fence across your path and then veer right to ford it. Then simply follow it down towards a prominent house and campsite. You will then reach a track at a point where both banks of the stream boast an assemblage of huge rocks.

Turn right onto the track and then simply walk and walk and walk . . . . for about 4km in fact along a track of varying surfaces and with excellent views rightward towards the hills you have climbed and left across the valley to the Carneddau. Pleasant enough, but unfortunately the gentle but persistent hum of traffic on the nearby A5 is hard to escape.

At length, and possibly you will consider that it is not before time you will come to the car park and, if you are driving back towards Bangor, you will probably now feel more lenient towards the ever so gentle hum your own car is generating.

Reverse Route This is a comparatively easy route to do in reverse: this would be preferable if the day is due to improve. From the initial track watch out for the bouldery stream mentioned at the end of the commentary above and start your climb along it ■

Note

The A5. This road was built in the 1820's by the famous Scottish engineer, Thomas Telford. The then existing road has been described as 'a miserable track, circuitous and craggy, full of terrible jolts, round bogs, and over rocks where horses broke their legs.' Telford's new road took eleven years to build, this lengthy time partly caused by bureaucracy, claims by landowners and so on (how little some things change!). It was worth the wait however, since acute curves had been straightened and steep sections reduced to not more than 5 per cent. The result was that mail coaches could speed along at 10 mph.

The road followed on from the construction of the port of Holyhead to link Great Britain to Ireland subsequent to the Act of Union between the two countries, which came into force in 1801. Irish members of parliament welcomed the new road because, with the Irish Parliament abolished, they had to travel to London and arrived there weary after the long journey. In addition the new road greatly aided commerce between North-West Wales and the rest of the country.

It still carries a lot of traffic though the A55, since its upgrading, takes most of the traffic bound for the east and south-east.

ROUTE 12: NANT PERIS TO ELIDIR FAWR

A climb through rough fields leads to a spur offering easy walking as far as the magnificent cliffs of the Glyderau range. A walk along these cliffs ends at Mynydd Perfedd (812m) from where a narrow ridge leads to Elidir Fawr: its challenging but avoidable bouldery ridge means slow and arduous progress. To finish a pleasant descent along the lower valley of the Afon Dudodyn.

Know Before You Go If rocks are likely to be wet avoid the boulders on Elidir Fawr by descending into the upper valley of Afon Dudodyn rather than tackle it.
Getting There Park in the large, free car park in Nant Peris (gr 6058). **Bus**: Use the frequent S1 bus service from Llanberis.
Walking Time 4.5 hours (distance 10km, climb 920m), this time including 30 minutes extra along the Elidir Fawr ridge.
Route Turn left from the car park, take the first turn right (signed 'Cae Gwyn') and cross the gate a little way up, where you should see an incongruous red phone box off to the left. Here prepare for a stiff climb up through rough fields on a right of way with minimal markings.

If you keep the initial stone wall on your left as you ascend you will be roughly on the right of way. You may be cheered to reach an Access Land sign a considerable distance up but unfortunately this access does not extend to the land on the left of the ascent route which is where you really want to be. Nothing for it therefore but to plod on and upward until a broken stile indicates a path down to the left towards tributaries of the Afon Gafr. Cross these and they climb immediately to the crest of the delightful rocky spur starting in gr 6159. Follow it north, so passing a set of sturdy sheep enclosures.

About ten minutes beyond these cross a **stile** and here, given that you have an option, consider what to do next. Note that there are few navigational terrors ahead as the Glyderau cliffs will call a halt to careless wandering, but remember also that progress is going to be slow along the Elidir Fawr ridge and that may be a factor. The variation is to climb directly from here to the bwlch directly south of Foel-goch (831m) and thence to the summit itself, so extending your walk by about 20 minutes, much of it along the cliffs. For the main route aim for Bwlch y Brecan to Foel-goch's north. In both cases, when you reach the Bwlch take the minor fork north at a path junction to reach Mynydd Perfedd (812m), whose summit shelter is reached by climbing a stile.

From Mynydd Perfedd descend south-west to a narrow bwlch above Marchlyn Mawr Reservoir [1], its smooth dam and obvious high water mark an unwelcome intrusion in this wild country. The bwlch is a good place to bail out if conditions are too difficult to tackle the rocks ahead; simply descend steeply south-east into the valley of Afon Dudodyn, surely the most boring mountain valley in Wales.

If you elect to go on keep along the crest of the bouldery ridge that is Elidir Fawr. The crest extends for about 1.5km and carries a path of sorts which stoutly traverses the short grassy patches and cravenly disappears over the long stretches of boulders.

At length, and by now you have been gradually descending for some time, the end of a wall will come into view on the left heading south down the slope into easier ground. Cross it where you can and head roughly south. The aim now is to reach Afon Dudodyn either upstream of, or at a footbridge at gr 608596, which leaves you plenty of scope to find your own way; just keep well clear of the immense quarry remains on the right. One way is to cross a stile, a wall and fence together on the right, and take the path beyond directly to the bridge.

Once across, take the track downstream; it unaccountably deteriorates to a narrow path and swings right at a ruin. Continue on the path down to a lane that ends at the A4086 with only a few minutes walk to the start.

Long Variation Follow the start of Route 10 to Llyn y Cŵn and then climb Y Garn and Foel-goch before rejoining the main route to tackle Mynydd Perfedd. This gives a lovely cliff-edge walk.

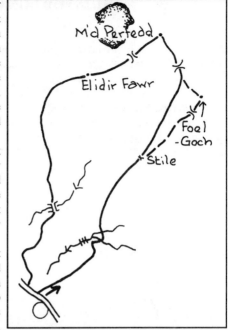

The total walking time is 5.75 hours (distance 13km, climb 1230m).

Note

1. This reservoir is the upper lake for the electricity pumped storage scheme called Dinorwig. The idea is that water is pumped up to here at night through underground pipes from a lower lake using lots of electricity and, during the day, the same water is allowed to cascade down through these pipes and so generate electricity – but less than has already been consumed. What's the point of that? you may well ask. Well, electricity cannot be stored so the most efficient generating stations are run day and night with the less efficient ones on load only over the daytime peaks. So the pumped storage scheme uses cheap electricity (at night) and allows the dearest generating stations to be kept off load during the day peaks.

THE SNOWDON GROUP

ROUTE 13: YR ARAN

A stiff climb of nearly 700m ends in shapely Yr Aran (747m), an unjustly neglected outlier of Snowdon/Yr Wyddfa. The return is along a rough ridge to Craig Wen and finally on a scenic but hardly memorable valley path. Perhaps too much climbing given the short stretch of high ground but nonetheless a good, varied walk.

Know Before You Go Lots of pathless, rough ground after Yr Aran where attention to the compass is advisable since you must find a fortuitously prominent farmhouse near Beddgelert.

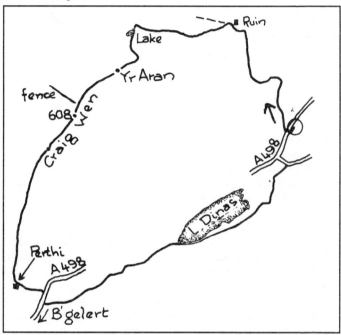

Getting There Park in the large, free car park (with toilets) just off the A498 at gr 6250. From Beddgelert this is about a half-mile beyond large Llyn Dinas; from Pen-y-Gwryd a little farther beyond even larger Llyn Gwynant. **Bus**: a poor service from Beddgelert and Betws-y-coed on route S97, but if you are based in Beddgelert you can start walking and pick up the route at the appropriate point.

Walking Time 4.5 hours (distance 13km, climb 750m).

Route Turn left out of the car park and take the first track on the right up through a wood and into open country with the waterfalls and cascades of Afon Cwm Llan a visual treat on the right. Just beyond a substantial **ruin** on the opposite bank you enter the much flatter upper valley of Cwm Llan and divert left onto a minor earth path. This shortly ends on an old mining rail line onto which you turn right over an impressive embankment. Follow the line for about 10 minutes and then take a faint path west and up.

The aim here is to reach the south (left) end of the bwlch to the right of Yr Aran, the high mountain to the south-west. One way to do this (among several) is to keep on the faint path until it joins a major one, continue up to a ruined wall, turn left to follow it and then make your way over or around a few minor bumps until you come to an east-west oriented **lake** about 25m long (15 double-steps) tucked into a narrow gully. This marks the start of the direct climb to Yr Aran.

There is a path all the way; it is easy to follow though it swings sharply left to avoid minor scree higher up before regaining its original direction. The summit furniture is unimpressive: a small cairn perched on a modest outcrop, but the views with Snowdon (north), Cnicht (south-east), Moel Hebog dominant to the south-west and the Nantlle Ridge to the west are excellent.

Descend south-west keeping a short stretch of cliffs on the right and following unemployed fence posts all the way down to the col facing Craig Wen (608m), where a sturdy **fence**, ending here and heading west might be a useful reassurance in bad weather. Craig Wen is really only a narrow plateau with two minor bumps along it. At the plateau's southern end you should reach a wall junction and think about the descent towards Beddgelert.

Much effort could be expended in describing this section of the route but it really amounts to this: your aim is the farmhouse Perthi at gr 589486 and to get there across the rough moorland country ahead follow any wall or intermittent path going south. At two points you will probably be slightly diverted to pass through gates rather than cross a wall. Having crossed the second gate you should be almost in sight of the imposing farmhouse and pick up a path, dipping right to left, running across steep ground.

Pass through a narrow and unaccommodating gate to the left of the farmhouse and then pick up a right of way running east and to the left of a rhododendron-infested hill. Take it to the road, the A498, turn right, turn shortly first left along a narrow public road and continue on its extension as a path past the Sygun Copper Mine building, now following the 'Lakeside Walk'. This leads along part of the length of Llyn Dinas before abandoning the shore to head into a wood. Path ends at track, track at narrow road, then a tee, where you turn left to reach the A498 again. Here turn right to the start only a few hundred metres along ■

ROUTE 14: PEN-Y-PASS, Y LLIWEDD AND SNOWDON

In distance a comparatively short approach to Snowdon but an exceptionally steep and scenic one: over the several summits of Y Lliwedd, then a demoralising drop, and finally an unrelenting climb to Snowdon's summit. After this exhilarating outward leg the return is anti-climactic along the all-too-manmade Pyg Track.

Know Before You Go There are a few places where very easy scrambling may be required but nothing worse than the first such. There is one punishingly steep descent. Other than a direct return, this is a route to which you are committed from near the start. Navigation is generally easy.

Getting There The start at the car park at Pen-y-Pass (gr 6455) is hardly ideal: it is expensive to leave a car there and it gets crowded early on popular days. The alternatives are to take your chances at several informal parking places around Pen-y-Gwryd (gr 6655) and walk up the road (about 20 minutes) or preferably leave your car at Nant Peris (gr 6058) and get the S1 bus to the start proper. **Bus:** S1 from Llanberis, S2 or S97 from Betws-y-coed.

Walking Time 4.25 hours (distance 11km, climb 930m).

Route Take the track south from the car park past Llyn Teyrn to the valve station at Llyn Lydaw and here branch left onto a path which climbs steeply to, and then

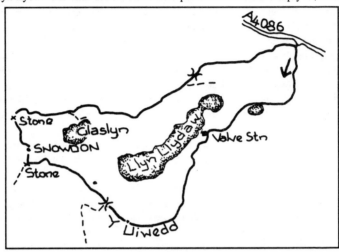

mainly just to the left of, the crests of the several rocky summits that constitute Y Lliwedd. Along this spur, among other delights lofty Moel Hebog is prominent off to the south-west. The last of these summits is the highest at 898m, so you are now only 200m below the summit of Snowdon. Which is all very encouraging were it not for the fact that you now face a cruel descent of over 150m to Bwlch Ciliau, initially on a stony zig-zag path and then on the partly paved Watkin Path winding up from Cwm Llan. The path through the Bwlch follows the left side of the crest and so avoids a rocky top that not many seem to have climbed.

From the Bwlch take the steep winding path through scattered stones and rocks on the now indeterminate crest as far as the **2m-high stone** that marks the right turn (to north) to the summit of Snowdon (1085m), the merits and demerits of which are expounded under Route 18[1].

From here on navigation is child's play and you will have plenty of company, whether you want to or not. Head north with the rail line to a **3m-high stone** and then turn right to head down the Pyg Track to its junction with the Miners' Track above Glaslyn, the first of two large lakes in the valley below and fronting the jagged peaks of Y Lliwedd climbed earlier. Here fork left to keep on the Pyg Track to another junction, this one above Llyn Lydaw. Fork left again to pass through the narrow Bwlch y Moch, where there is a double stile and a refreshingly different view, the steep-sided Pass of Llanberis. Initially keep a fence on the left to head east on a clear path or track all the way back to Pen-y-Pass ■

Notes

1. A new restaurant is a present (2008) being constructed on the summit at a whopping cost of £8.35m, three times what it would cost if it were constructed at sea level. The extra cost is accounted for by its location at over 1000m: it has to withstand winds of 150 mph, 200 inches of rain per year and temperatures of –20 degrees C.

The mountain railway from Llanberis was constructed in an amazing 13 months in 1896. Ironically its opening on Easter Day was marred by the only accident leading to a fatality in its long history. A train was returning from the summit when the engine left the line and crashed over a cliff. A passenger in one of the carriages jumped clear but died later of his injuries.

ROUTE 15: MOEL EILIO AND MOEL CYNGHORION

A long walk over easy terrain along Snowdon's broad north-west spur, with a return well before that summit. A dull start improves to give excellent views over cliffs down into the remote valley of the Afon Arddu with a return along this valley. Except for near the end, easy walking underfoot.

Know Before You Go Navigation is not too difficult though some points along the upland section require attention. A short stretch near the end is horribly wet underfoot. It is easy to shorten the route.

Getting There Start in the town of Llanberis. There is usually plenty of free parking along the A4086, which skirts the village. **Bus:** There is a good bus service from Caernarfon to Llanberis.

Walking Time 5.25 hours (distance 14km, climb 1020m).

Route From Stryd Fawr, the town's main street, turn into Stryd Ceunant and just beyond the youth hostel take a track on the right and then the first stile on the left. Keep heading south-west and uphill, walking where you can to the left of the wide spur for excellent views down into Llyn Dwythwch. As you near the crest of the spur reaching north from Moel Eilio you will join a wider path onto which you turn (surprise, surprise) uphill. There are good coastal views here towards Anglesey and the mountains of Lleyn Peninsula to its left.

Moel Eilio (726m) has a shelter and offers good views but its summit, like all others on this route, is hardly memorable. From here on keep the cliffs close on the left, both for easy navigation and because of the fine views on this side.

The cliffs continue over Foel Gron (629m), which has two tops about 500m apart, and Foel Goch (605m), where you have to make a slight detour left over a stile to reach the summit.

On the descent from Foel Goch cliffs on the left ease so you may have to rely on your compass to head south with a touch of east, though once you keep a fence off on your right you cannot go too far wrong. You won't mistake Bwlch Maesgwm at pt 467m (gr 572558) since a high stone wall and a wide track heading left and valley-ward converge here and it is the site of much mountain furniture. A good place to abandon the walk if conditions are deteriorating.

Moel Cynghorion (674m) is the last mountain. Keep the fence on the left all the way to the soggy summit. After it, swing sharply to south-east, cliff close on the left to reach the nearby bwlch. You will know you are there as you will see a steep rocky rise close

ahead and the wide Snowdon Ranger Path just below you. From here it's nearly all downhill. Cross the fence and head north into the valley of the Afon Arddu, one overlooked by stern, rocky ground. Keep the developing stream on the right and simply follow it on an intermittent path.

About 2km down you will come to a spur projecting to what is now a comparatively wide river on the right. Climb the spur and contour along the wall beyond it for 200m or so, and then cross a stile over it. Walk through rough ground to the right of a house that gives a new dimension to the real estate agent's phrase 'a quiet location, not overlooked'. Take the dreadfully potholed and muddy track beyond it to reach a narrow road, pass under the railway bridge and follow your nose back into Llanberis ■

ROUTE 16: GALLT Y WENALLT AND Y LLIWEDD

A route of varied thirds: the first up through woodland and partly pathless open country overlooking a lovely terrain of lake and wooded valley, the second an exhilarating walk along the edge of cliffs climaxing in lofty Y Lliwedd (898m) and the third a gradual descent through a somewhat dull valley and back through the initial woods.

Know Before You Go The first third of the route, being partly pathless, requires attention to navigation. It is easy enough to extend this route to Snowdon itself but not so easy to shorten it.

Getting There As in Route 13.

Walking Time 4.25 hours (distance 11km, climb 900m).

Route Turn left out of the car park and take the first track on the right up through a wood and into open country until you are close to the waterfalls and cascades of Afon Cwm Llan. Cross a prominent bridge below an equally prominent waterfall and take the path beyond it, crossing a stile ahead (not the one on the left) a little way up.

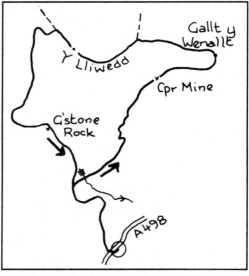

Continue up and north-east through woods and beyond into open country, at one stage coming through a tiny gap to see the distinct Gallt y Wenallt ahead; indeed looking so distinct that when you actually reach its indeterminate summit you may wonder if it is the same mountain. For now, continue on the path to eventually cross a gate on the left. Immediately beyond it turn left and swing right to walk a clear, grassy track heading up in a leisurely fashion.

Even though the track begins to descend disconcertingly keep with it to reach old copper mine workings; others are sprawled up the slope. It is here, with a remote and rough high valley before you, that real navigational problems start.

The idea is to reach the summit of Gallt y Wenallt, such as it is, though in bad conditions it might be better to abandon this summit and head for the crest of the Y Lliwedd ridge. Even in good weather a bearing of about 80° might be a good idea. With this bearing, cross a tiny area of scree, follow a wall as long as it is heading roughly in the correct direction and then a tumbled wall and fence ambling up the far bank of an infant stream flowing west.

At its source you are close to the southern end of the summit of Gallt y Wenallt

(619m) with spectacular views over the woods and lakes of Nant Gwynant.

After you have abandoned the search for the definitive summit of the elusive Gallt y Wenallt and you are walking west with steep ground overlooking Cwm Dyli on the right, navigational problems are behind, though considerable expenditure of energy is now called for. Consolation: this is a highly memorable stretch with terrific views from a cliff edge down into an upland cwm and across to Crib Goch, the most (in)famous of Snowdon's spurs.

It's easily described: continue west over both of Y Lliwedd's two subsidiary summits, leaving the clear path to reach the cliff edge if you have the energy and head for heights, and then climb sharp-topped Y Lliwedd (898m), a summit with views that are nothing short of spectacular.

Even in the worst conditions you cannot miss Y Lliwedd, or rather the steep, difficult, rock-strewn path beyond it which will land you on the partly man-made Watkin Path. This winds up from the wide and rather featureless upper valley of Cwm Llan with its impressive stone buildings and ugly abandoned mine workings [1] Keep on the Path right down through the upper valley, passing Gladstone Rock [2] on the way (the plaque to the Grand Old Man faces down-valley so you may have to search around a bit to find it).

At length you will make the descent into the wooded country where you started. There is only one point to watch out for here: fork right in the wood rather than come to grief in private grounds. After which you should have no bother in finding your way back to the car park ∎

Notes

1. As many walks in Snowdonia amply demonstrate much quarrying has been undertaken in the mountains in the past. Cwm Llan and the area on the other side of Nant Gwynant (where there is an interpretative centre giving the history of mining here) was pre-eminently an area of copper mines. All the mines started up in the mid-1700's and lasted for about a century. There were three copper mines (lead and slate were also extracted) in this immediate area along with water mills and rolling ore crushers, a miners' barracks and other ancillary buildings. Route 13 follows the route of a rail line heading along the south-west side of the valley, though what it was used for is not known exactly.

2. In 1892 the Watkin Path was presented to the State for public use by Sir Edward Watkin. He persuaded the prime minister, William Gladstone, to officially open it. Gladstone, 'The Grand Old Man', an epithet he merited since he was then 84, duly arrived in the pouring rain in an open carriage (no slogging it on foot for him) and spoke about justice for the Welsh and the question of land ownership. Strangely, he did not once mention the Watkin Path, the ostensible reason for his visit.

ROUTE 17: LLANBERIS TO NEAR SNOWDON

This route does not take in Snowdon or the all-too-popular Llanberis Path but it does come close to both. The outward leg follows the crest of a rising, undulating spur overlooking the rugged Pass of Llanberis. The return is along a spur running from near Snowdon and then down a mountain remote valley. Excellent scenery throughout but little sense of remoteness.

Know Before You Go At any point in the first half of the walk you can drop down to the Llanberis Path. The second half, from the point where you leave the rail tracks is less accommodating, though there is one easy escape route. Navigation is easy in the first half and not too difficult in the second. It is very easy to include Snowdon's summit if you wish: simply follow the rail tracks.

Getting There Park in Llanberis, where there is free parking along the lakeshore. Llanberis is well served by buses.

Walking Time 6 hours (distance 17km, climb 1050m).

Route Follow the numerous signs in the rail terminal end of the town for 'Snowdon Footpaths'. These will take you under the railway line and steeply uphill on tarmac. Leave the road at the sign on the left 'Snowdon Summit' but do not take the indicated Llanberis Path. Instead the plan from here on is to keep cliffs and steep ground directly on the left, enjoy the excellent views down and along the Pass of Llanberis (that is once you get past the dreadful slate quarries looming over the town), and scorn the dogged souls toiling up the Llanberis Path.

So first climb pathlessly to Derlwyn (403m), drop slightly

to cross a stile beyond it and continue up and south-east. A warning: on this next steep ascent keep the fence on the left even though it somewhat limits the views; the ground between cliff and fence narrows alarmingly farther up and there is no easy place to cross it (my wounds are healing nicely – thanks for asking).

After this climb it's straightforward all the way over the boulders of Llechog (718m) and then to the unfortunately unavoidable mountain railway just short of Clogwyn Station. There is no getting away from the tracks as it swings sharply right but when after about 20 minutes from the Station it swings left and ascends it is time to bid it farewell and head west to meet the cliffs overlooking Llyn Du'r Arddu on the right.

Along here it is easy to pick up the wide Snowdon Ranger Path and take it down, but it is more rewarding to negotiate the heaps of boulders underfoot close to the cliff edge – these are especially difficult in the initial stages. Once beyond them, and you are now on the crest of a spur plunging valley-ward on the right, you can enjoy the views down into the upper valley of the Afon Arddu, where you are eventually headed.

The spur ends in a deep bwlch at gr 591557 with the Snowdon Ranger Path just off to the left. Here you can cut the walk short by less than a half hour by descending north into the upper valley (more details under Route 15) but if you haven't already done so it is worthwhile climbing Moel Cynghorion (674m) for the views it gives over the cliffs. It's a simple climb north-west from the bwlch, after which you turn west over easy grass to meet the walls, gate, paths and stiles at the next bwlch. No mistaking it!

Turn right downhill here onto a clear path. You can either walk all the way down straight into Llanberis on this path and its gradually improving and widening extension or take a slightly more subtle route as you near the town. For the latter walk what is now a track past a few houses and then look out for what appears to be a **blockhouse** of some kind on the left. Just beyond it divert right off the track onto a vague path and pass through a semi-circular gate on the left to walk close by a house on the right. From here you can easily find your way down into the town ∎

ROUTE 18: SNOWDON FROM THE WEST

Two well-beaten paths partway to and from Snowdon's summit . . . but with a diversion. The ascent starts on the Snowdon Ranger Path but transfers to the Rhyd-Ddu Path by walking cross-country taking in a remote and splendid corrie. Snowdon's summit and its approach offer great views, though the descent, the Ranger Path, is a trifle tame.

Know Before You Go Some navigational care needed off the two main paths.

Getting There Park in the Snowdon Ranger car park (gr 5655) opposite the hostel about 7 miles south of Caernarfon. **Bus**: S4 from Caernarfon or Beddgelert.

Walking Time 4.75 hours (distance 12km, climb 1000m).

Route Cross the road and take the clear Snowdon Ranger Path until, after nearly 3km, you are approaching Llyn Ffynnon-y-gwas, a large lake close to the Path. Leave it here, and keeping the lake on the left head south-east towards a cascade issuing from Llyn Coch. Follow the cascade, keeping it and a sturdy barbed-wire **fence** on the right as you climb the steep slope to the corrie, Cwm Clogwyn. When you reach it cross the fence by a stile and the outlet stream on rudimentary stepping stones.

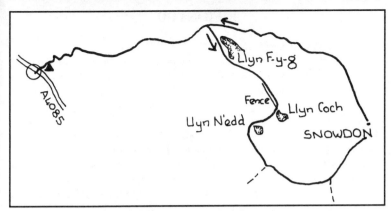

This is a magnificent location with the lake hemmed in by stern boulder-strewn crags. Of the two other lakes perched above Llyn Coch it is to the one to the west, Llyn Nadroedd, that beckons. Cross the latter's outlet stream, where there is unaccountably some stonework, and then climb along the crest of the partly grassy, partly rocky spur south to the Rhyd-Ddu Path, which you cannot mistake since, not only is it wide and eroded, but there are unnecessary cairns along it.

Curiously the Path is much more attractive farther up where it runs initially as a narrow path with a steep drop to the left and nearer Snowdon's summit along a narrow ridge.

The summit (1085m) is impossible to miss, what with the terminus of the mountain railway, the restaurant, and the hordes of day-trippers. If you can stomach all that you cannot fail to be impressed by the location: to the south Yr Aran, the specially impressive jagged Y Lliwedd to the south-east, the great valley sheltering Llyn Llydaw and other lakes to its left, with Crib Goch farther left again. Farther off to the west are the Nantlle Ridge and Moel Hebog, roughly to the west and south-west respectively.

From Snowdon head north with the throngs with the rail line on the left. But not indefinitely: after 10 minutes or so cross the tracks and follow the Snowdon Ranger Path all the way down to the start. Remember though that like so many popular paths it eschews the best views. With this in mind you might like to keep the Path on the left and walk the crest of the ridge over bouldery ground as far as the bwlch at gr 591557. From there down there is no realistic option but to keep to the Path. At least there's no possibility of getting lost! ■

EIFIONYDD

ROUTE 19: THE NANTLLE RIDGE

For most of its length this is a superb and exhilarating narrow ridge walk running between admittedly undistinguished peaks. Some easy scrambling and boulder-hopping add to the zest. The close-up views are superb though the farther ones change only slowly, one consequence of a linear route. Incidentally, for what it's worth, if I were to recommend just one walk in North Snowdonia, this would be it.

Know Before You Go This is an A to B route, so there may be logistical problems. Navigation generally requires some attention though it is not too difficult. It is a toss-up whether to do the walk as here, east to west, or in reverse; the given direction has the advantage that the two steepest sections – one bouldery – are ascents. If you want an escape route revert to the easier variation of Route 20. The map for this route is given in Routes 20 and 21.

Getting There Park one car in the informal parking place at gr 483499. This is reached by taking the A487 south from Penygroes, then follow signs for Nebo, but 0.3 miles after the sign Nebo ^{1}/2, fork right and continue to the parking place 0.7 miles further on. Take the second car back to Penygroes, turn right here onto the B4418 and drive to Rhyd-Ddu. Turn right into the village and park in the car park at its end (charge).

If you haven't a second car do not despair. Ring Hughes Taxi, preferably the day before, at 01286-676767 and make an arrangement with them. If you are based in Caernarfon you could use the S4 bus to Rhyd-Ddu and the 1A back from Nebo.

Walking Time 6 hours (distance 13km, climb 1040m) including about an hour over Naismith to allow for boulder fields and at least one steep descent.

Route From the car park take the signposted right of way on the other side of the road and, chivvied by numerous paint marks, arrows and 'keep out' signs make your way almost to the B4418. Here follow the signs west and head for all too looming and from here dominant Y Garn (633m). To get there take a well-worn path; at one point it passes close to cliffs. Evade as best you can a boulder field near the summit, cross a stile over a wall even nearer it and so reach what look like shelters on the summit plateau but which the OS describes as cairns.

From Y Garn keep cliffs close on the right to follow a wall south to the boulders guarding Mynydd Drws-y-coed (695m); it's a not so gentle climb and the heaped boulders may cause some back-tracking and certainly demand careful attention. Normal conditions resume just before the indistinct summit where the **end of a fence** heading downward left may be a useful landmark in bad conditions.

Next Trum y Ddysgl (709m). Descend from Mynydd Drws-y-coed on a clear path initially south along a grassy ridge, but then swing right to pass the bwlch between the summits, *take care to branch right onto a minor rising path* rather than contour below Trum y Ddysgl.

It's hard to imagine a more modest summit than that of Trum y Ddysgl: short grass without even a decent cairn. Since the next summit, Mynydd Tal-y-mignedd, is crowned by a mighty obelisk clearly visible for miles around in all but the worst conditions, the way ahead is obvious. However should you be so unfortunate as to be here in cloud, *take the south-west ridge from Trum y Ddysgl and fork right after 200m or so where the ridge divides* (fork left here as an escape route or if you are walking the eastern end of the Nantlle Ridge only: this is one option given in Route 20). This ridge is only a few metres wide; the views on both sides are spectacular. From the **obelisk** on Mynydd Tal-y-mignedd (653m) follow a fence and a grassy ridge south and where the fence terminates continue south-west and steeply downhill to the spectacular Bwlch Dros-bern (about 532507), overlooking mountain valleys to right and left and with the awe-inducing climb through crags to Craig Cwm Silyn ahead. In the Bwlch incidentally are a few sturdy fence posts, maybe a useful landmark in really bad conditions.

Walk to the far end of the Bwlch and then climb steeply on a not too intermittent path to the large cairn with a square cross-section close to the summit of Craig Cwm Silyn, at 734m the highest point on the route; it is the near end of a mostly grassy plateau about 1.5km long. The views from Craig Cwm Silyn are really memorable: the Nantlle Ridge stretching away to the east, beyond it the Snowdon massif and to the south-east Moel Hebog dominating the skyline.

Rather than take the direct route to Garnedd-goch at the far end of the plateau, you might like to veer right of this line to take in the great corrie holding the two Llynnau Cwm Silyn and then return to the spine of the plateau, initially following a wall and crossing a boulder field close to the partly decayed remains of a trig pillar on the summit (700m).

This summit is surrounded by boulders, walls, and stiles; since it barely rises above the general level of the plateau it would be difficult to locate exactly were it not for this pillar. I'm not sure why the mountain's name is given in ancient Gothic print indicating something of archaeological interest; there seems to be nothing here to warrant this.

From here walk roughly south while trying to avoid patches of boulder field and high heather to the **corner of a wall** at gr 510489. At this point you may like to forego the last summit, Mynydd Graig Goch. To do this head west from the corner of the wall and so enter a narrow valley. At its end keep Llyn Cwm Dulyn on the left to reach the end of the track mentioned below. This reduces the walking time by about 15 minutes and navigational strain by an unquantifiable but possibly considerable amount. However if you elect to go on, head west over rough, pathless ground, passing a cairn on a boulder base 1km from the summit, whose exact purpose I cannot fathom.

'Summit' may not be the word to describe the any of the would-be highest points on Mynydd Graig Goch (609m), which is a maze of boulders and sections of stout stone wall running between and among them. The best you can do is to head resolutely west among these obstacles until you are beyond them and can swing right (north-west) along a steep spur above Llyn Cwm Dulyn. As you approach the shores of the lake look out for the end of a track that will keep you out of the worst of the rushy country hereabouts. Walk from here to the parking place a few hundred metres ahead ■

ROUTE 20: THE EASTERN NANTLLE RIDGE

The first half is a spectacular ridge walk, probably the best of that outlined under Route 19. The return is partly through old mining settlements and partly through forest. If you cannot do the entire Nantlle Ridge (Route 19) this is the next best.

Know Before You Go There is a stretch of boulder-hopping and -climbing to the second summit. Pay attention to navigation around the mining area with complicated topography after you descend from the Nantlle Ridge.

Getting There Park in the car park (considerable charge) in the village of Rhyd-Ddu on the A4085 about 9 miles south of Caernarfon. **Bus:** S4 from Caernarfon and S97 from Betws-y-coed or Porthmadog.

Walking Time 3.5 hours (distance 9km, climb 720m), but allow some time to explore the mine working area (see below).

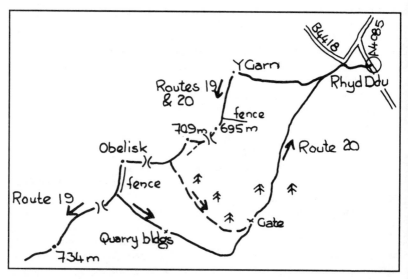

Route As in Route 19 walk to just beyond the obelisk on Mynydd Tal-y-mignedd (653m), after it following a grassy ridge carrying a fence. Where the fence terminates bid farewell to the Nantlle Ridge.

Descend a grassy spur running south-east and, veering left off the crest as you reach its end, watch out for the ruins of quarry buildings down in the tiny valley of Cwm Dwyfor. Head for the lowest of these buildings, cross the valley's stream avoiding a very soggy area as best you can, and then follow a tumbled wall roughly east up hill and down dale (it disappears at one point). Incidentally, that's wooded Cwm Pennant stretching away to the right, with the craggy shoulder of the northern extension of Moel Lefn coming into view ahead.

Less than 1km from Cwm Dwyfor you have the option of exploring the mining area below the wall. To do so, divert from it where you see an extensive area of spoil below you but remember how to return to it. This area is well worth a leisurely amble since it vividly brings back the mining era. That done, return to the wall and where it shortly meets a track contouring around a narrow valley, turn left onto it, keeping straight ahead (north) on a good path where the track swings sharply right. Still on the path, cross a gate (gr 552503) fronting a few scattered trees, where the easy variation (see below) rejoins.

Take the path into forest to a track, turn right and immediately left onto another track. At a tee, cross the bridge on the left and immediately turn right onto a path. This will take you directly beyond forest and also beyond tedious directions: simply follow the appropriate path all the way roughly north into Rhyd-Ddu.

Navigationally Easy Variation From the obelisk return east across the narrow ridge and just before the climb to Trum y Ddysgl swing right onto the crest of a south-east running spur with forest below and off to the left. Come gradually off the crest to cross the gate at gr 552503; then follow the directions above ■

ROUTE 21: THE WESTERN NANTLLE RIDGE

A cross-country slog over rough terrain ends above the twin Cwm Silyn lakes. A stiff but scenic climb follows along a cliff-edge to the first of three boulder-strewn summits offering excellent views over mountain and seascapes.

Know Before You Go The first part of the route requires attention to navigation, because if you don't you might have problems finding the rest of it. There are a few easily negotiated bouldery sections.

Getting There Start at the finishing point of Route 19 at gr 483499.

Walking Time 3.5 hours (distance 10km, climb 640m).

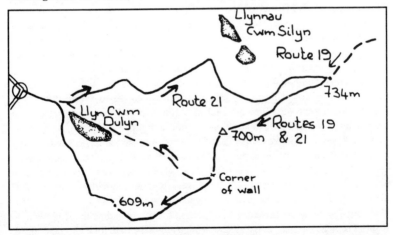

Route The first objective is to get near Lynnau Cwm Silyn by keeping above enclosed fields. The details (for reassurance): from the car park walk east along the track over a sturdy footbridge and immediately after cross a stile on the right. Walk upwards to cross another stile. Turn left here to follow a fence and wall forming the upper boundary of an upland field. A short distance along turn right at a gate to follow a rough grassy track upward beside a field improbably harbouring two tiny copses.

Where the wall turns left, leave the track to follow it - it's the upper boundary of enclosed land - over rather boggy ground. Carefully cross a wall ahead without damaging either it or yourself and then follow a contouring fence. At its far end you are within a few hundred metres of Lynnau Cwm Silyn and much more rewarding and navigationally easy terrain lies ahead.

Your target now is the fine grassy spur immediately to your south that plunges on its left into the corrie enclosing the lakes. Keep close to the corrie edge as you ascend and partway along the plateau above. This is a delightful stretch: the rocky cliffs tumbling below to the lakes are a pleasing contrast to the moorland walked so far.

Once on the plateau the aim is to reach Craig Cwm Silyn (734m), situated at the plateau's eastern end and the highest mountain in the entire Nantlle Ridge. To reach it walk to a fine partly tumbled square-sectioned ruin, turn right at it, and pass several more to one almost at the summit. But not quite, since the actual summit and the point where those on Route 19 meet us is 150m farther on at a rough shelter. Not an impressive summit, but the views are splendid.

From here follow the directions under Route 19 all the way to the finish. Just one point: as you start out you might like to keep to the left of the plateau for views to wooded Cwm Pennant rather than repeat the section along the cliff edge above Llynnau Cwm Silyn ∎

ROUTE 22: MYNYDD MAWR

A delightful, all too short route offering splendid views over the higher peaks of Snowdonia. Underfoot conditions are mostly good though navigation may be difficult in parts. Two downsides: a lot of climbing for not so much high-level walking and a road walk, some of which is avoidable with two cars.

Know Before You Go Without two cars or the occasional bus you face 3.5km of road walk. The somewhat featureless plateau between the two tops of Mynydd Mawr may present some navigational difficulties in bad visibility. Under such conditions it may be better to leave out the northern top.

Getting There Park in the car park (gr 5655) opposite the Snowdon Ranger hostel on the A4085 about 7 miles south-east of Caernarfon. If you have a second car you can park it carefully on the side of the road about 5½ miles from Caernarfon, where a sign just ahead reads Plas-y-nant. **Bus:** S4 from Caernarfon or Beddgelert; the bus has the great advantage that you can omit the road walk.

Walking Time 4 hours (distance 12km, climb 620m), including the road walk.

Route From the car park turn right and trudge along the road for a kilometre or so, here taking the first right. Cross the gate warning of bears ahead and bear (catching, isn't it?) immediately left onto an uphill path. Continue on it through forest, crossing at length a rutted track to keep on what is now a steeply climbing path. Farther up you will come to a sign on a stile indicating that you are now entering Access Land: from here you can forget about navigation, concentrate on rapidly widening scenic views and ease your feet on a delightful grassy sward.

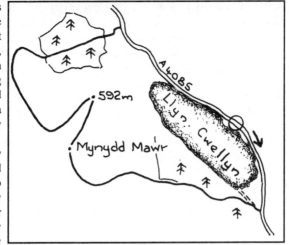

Your path now heads uphill and roughly west onto an increasingly impressive spur with the rocky cliffs of Craig y Bera on the left, the Nantlle ridge prominent beyond the narrow valley running between Nantlle and Rhyd-Ddu, and another valley, devoid of any features, interesting or otherwise, on the right.

After over a kilometre from entering Access Land the path bears away from the cliffs and heads for Mynydd Mawr (698m), an undistinguished summit of recumbent rocks, three shelters and a cairn.

Now for the northern top (592m) reached directly over easy though mostly pathless ground. Another cairn here and with cliffs just ahead overlooking the valley containing Llyn Cwellyn, quite a dramatic location. You should be easily able to see Caernarfon Castle to the north-west – plus of course the northern end of the Snowdon massif culminating in Snowdon itself off to the east.

Keep to the west (right) of your outward path from top 592m so aiming to overlook the cliffs and valley to the north. This involves some ascent and descent and walking rough and not particularly helpful paths. However the narrow gullies and strange rock formations near the tops of the cliffs make this stretch well worthwhile.

Swing right with the cliffs and you will come to a clear path heading north-west and downhill. Five minutes or so after you pass a small enclosed area of old mine workings take the right fork onto a narrow path. This will take you down to a rough path paralleling a stone wall some tens of metres off to the left (if you are going in the correct direction) with the stern cliffs of Craig Cwmbychan increasingly dominant ahead.

As you approach forest look out for a yellow arrow, a stile and a gap in the wall, all together. Plunge into dense forest here heading roughly east on a muddy path. Out of forest turn left onto a right of way that takes you across a railway line and onto the road, the A4085 of course. If you are lucky enough to have a car here, be thankful. Otherwise it's a trudge of about 2km along the road, which would be attractive were it not for the volume of traffic it carries. Maybe some kind driver who has also invested in this book will take pity on you! ∎

ROUTE 23: BEDDGELERT TO MOEL HEBOG

A memorable route of contrasting thirds. The first is a long and absorbing climb to the summit of Moel Hebog (782m), an isolated and imposing peak. The second is an exhilarating, undulating walk along two of Moel Hebog's rocky satellites. And the last? It's a varied route through trees and rough lowland country. However navigation is so complex that you might have little time to admire the scenery.

Know Before You Go There is a little easy scrambling near the summit of Moel Hebog. The navigational complexity of the last third of the route is described in copious (but maybe not copious enough) detail below.

Getting There Start in the village of Beddgelert. There is a free car park on the left as you enter the village on the A4085 from Rhyd-Ddu. **Bus**: S4 from Caernarfon and possibly S97 from Betws-y-coed.

Walking Time 4.75 hours (distance 12km, climb 1040m) in theory, but it might be prudent to add some time for route-finding in the last third.

Map The standard sheet 115 is barely sufficient for the last third of the route so the sketch map given here may be of some use.

Route Turn right out of the car park, walk a few hundred metres uphill and take the first road left (described as private). Continue uphill to the last farm and here turn right onto a track at a

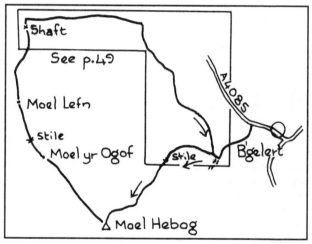

storage building. Fork shortly left onto a rough path following yellow arrows and then keep on it west and then south-west so that you are heading up a long, wide, rocky spur. Curiously the path is more indistinct lower down but is quite clear when you reach the last **stile** high up on the hillside at gr 574479. Which is just as well since you have to keep to it farther up.

This is because the last part of the climb is part steep path, part scree, part clambering over boulders. Then suddenly you are on a tiny, grassy plateau heralded by two large cairns. A short clamber over more rocks and a few minutes easy walk south on short grass and you are at the summit trig pillar (782m). It's a great viewpoint since Moel Hebog is surrounded by much lower peaks, so that the view encompasses in turn the Nantlle Ridge (north-west), the Snowdon massif (north-east), Moel Siabod (east) and Cnicht to its right. Now, wasn't it worth the effort!

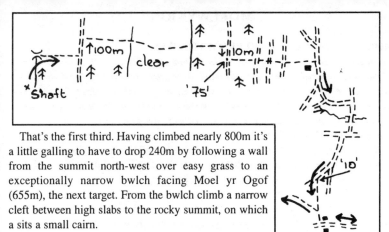

That's the first third. Having climbed nearly 800m it's a little galling to have to drop 240m by following a wall from the summit north-west over easy grass to an exceptionally narrow bwlch facing Moel yr Ogof (655m), the next target. From the bwlch climb a narrow cleft between high slabs to the rocky summit, on which a sits a small cairn.

Until the steep descent off this ridge nearly 3km north of here the views are predictably impressive with rumpled, partly forested country and lakes off to the right and the Nantlle Ridge prominent ahead and to the left. Enjoy!

On the rocky descent from Moel yr Ogof you may encounter a few errant fir trees, one bizarrely wedged into the summit boulders. That's one navigational aid but better is the **stile** with a wall on one side and a fence on the other at gr 555480. Which leaves Moel Lefn (638m), another rocky peak with a small cairn and worth climbing even though the path passes to its left. Heading north from its summit pick up a narrow earth path heading down initially diagonally right. It then steepens through a terrain of rocky ribs and boulders with the crest of what is now an indefinite spur a few hundred metres off to the left.

When you reach a **deep mine shaft** (gr 553494), please pay careful attention to the following dismal dirge to avoid (or more accurately reduce the chances of) getting lost.

Part I. Keeping forest close on the right descend steeply, at the nearby narrow bwlch turn right over a simple stile and head into forest on a clear path. At a forest track turn left, walk less than 100m and take a path on the right. Still on the path, emerge from forest into rough open ground, re-enter forest via another simple stile, walk to a forest track, turn right for 10m and at a post marked '75', turn left onto your path again. Cross a track three times and descend through a field to the left of a house to reach a rough road. Turn right.

Part II. Ignore minor tracks to continue down the road and so walk parallel to a wide stream on the right. At the tee turn right to reach a caravan park, where you might like to bail out and walk over 1km along the A4085 to the start. Otherwise turn right at the park, cross the rail line, immediately take the first track left, and ignore a minor grassy track on the right. *Fork right uphill at a barrier (where instinct says 'left downhill')* and then fork left onto a path with a '10' marker. Follow blue markers back to the initial storage building, lick your wounds and head for Beddgelert ■

MOELWYNION

ROUTE 24: MOEL SIABOD FROM THE WEST

To begin a delightful terrain of rocky hummocks ends in cliffs above isolated Llynnau Duweunydd. After it a dull climb over grass, relieved by excellent views, ends at the unexpectedly bouldery stand-alone summit of Moel Siabod. The descent to Pen-y-Gwryd is through moorland but the end on tracks and minor roads is down through highly scenic, varied Nantgwynant.

Know Before You Go This could be a tricky route navigationally in bad weather with two turning points to be made in virtually pathless and indistinct terrain, though the fence junction at gr 676543 (noted below) is useful. However if you still get lost there is always a reachable road close by.

Getting There There are several informal parking places at, or south of, Pen-y-Gwryd (gr 6555). If you start in bad conditions and think (or hope) that they are going to improve start at Pen-y-Gwryd and so initially walk a track valley-ward and away from the gloomy tops. Otherwise start at gr 657526 about 2 miles to the south on the A498 and just after a bridge. Parking here is on the right; there is a footpath sign on the left. **Bus**: possibly S97 from Betws-y-coed or Beddgelert.

Walking Time 5.25 hours (distance 15km, climb 920m).

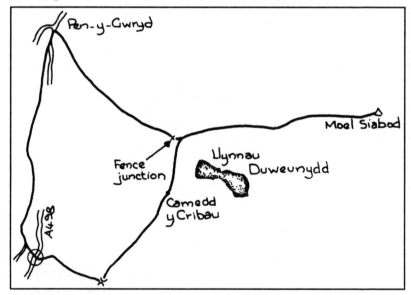

Route Take the footpath through a scattered deciduous wood into open country, pass a ruin on the left, shortly ignore a minor path heading right and at a shallow bwlch with a stile ahead, turn left onto pathless hills.

From here until you are above Llynnau Duweunydd nearly 2km to the north you traverse a region of rocky hillocks, up and down, with more up. It's enchanting – and made even better by excellent views leftward over the Snowdon massif. This

50

rugged country continues without break to Carnedd y Cribau (591m) where you have to cross a stile on the right to reach the large boulder marking the summit. Then a grassy descent north, and a last rocky hillock, Clogwyn Bwlch-y-maen overlooking Lynnau Duweunydd. Along here you might note off to your left a **fence junction** and two stiles at gr 676543; from here you will head for Pen-y-Gwryd on your return. After Clogwyn Bwlch-y-maen swing east, and walk directly to the summit of Moel Siabod on a broad spur over short grass ending in an unexpected area of boulders before the summit trig pillar (872m).

The descent is initially the same as the ascent: boulders; followed by the broad, grassy spur; but then you might like to bypass Clogwyn Bwlch-y-maen on your left to reach the fence junction nearly encountered earlier. From here head directly north-west to Pen-y-Gwryd over a strange terrain of soggy bog interspersed with bold rocky outcrops. Curiously, the buildings at Pen-y-Gwryd, visible from afar, disappear below the moorland closer to, so you may need a compass bearing to take you safely to the road just to the left of the buildings.

Walk south along the A498 for a few metres and then fork right onto a gravel track which farther down becomes a narrow tarmaced road, both however offering excellent views over wooded Nantgwynant. After about 1km on tarmac look out for a discreet sign on the left and follow it steeply uphill to the start ■

ROUTE 25: MOEL SIABOD FROM THE NORTH

This approach to Moel Siabod (872m) from Capel Curig is by a steep, rocky climb with some very mild scrambling before the summit and the traverse of a boulder field after it. Much of the route offers excellent long-distance views, especially towards the Snowdon massif.

Know Before You Go There is lots of boulder climbing (or evading) before the summit and boulder hopping after it.

Getting There The start is off the A5 between the villages of Capel Curig and Betws-y-coed at the free car park on the left (coming from Capel Curig) and signed Bryn Glô (gr 736572). **Bus**: S6 from Bethesda; S2, S6 and S97 from Betws-y-coed; S97 from Porthmadog.

Walking Time 4.25 hours (distance 10km, climb 760m), including about an additional half-hour for boulder climbing.

Route From the car park turn right onto the A5, take the first turn left over a bridge and beyond walk a narrow road. Ignore the first turn on the right and several tempting driveways and take the second turn right, which is signposted as a right of way, climbs steeply uphill as a rough, bouldery track and has a house wedged between tarmac and track. Can't miss it (I hope).

The track winds upward through deciduous trees and emerges in open moorland with fine views to Moel Siabod. Keep south to cross another track and later enter dense forest. Ignore the first track right in forest and take the second only a few metres farther on. Disconcertingly, this track makes no serious attempt to climb, even when you reach a tee and turn right. At the track's end cross a footbridge, turn

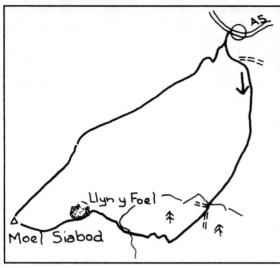

right immediately and prepare for a long-deferred struggle.

Take the rough, winding path, its route here and there blocked by fallen trees, steeply uphill and west through forest to emerge near the forest's higher edge. Cross a stream on the right after 150m or less, so keeping on a path through high vegetation that heads directly upward past a few small waterfalls. At their top, and here there is an unexpected stone dam, you will be suddenly confronted by the dramatic corrie lake of Llyn y Foel. Time for a well-deserved breather.

The way ahead is now clear: the rocky spur heading west from the lake. You will have to pick your way a little carefully along its crest or close to it while enjoying the excellent, expanding views, including a lot of wooded country beyond the Crimea Pass road.

At length and with little warning, the slope eases and the trig pillar marking the summit appears. From it there are magnificent views not only over much of the country walked so far but also across to the Snowdon massif to the west and the Glyderau to the north-west.

Next the rocky summit ridge, extending north-east for over two kilometres and offering views over rocky cliffs on the right, reaching down to boggy country beyond Llyn y Foel. This is slow going and will probably involve some undignified sliding down smooth rocks but in no case too far for you to come to grief. After roughly 20 minutes you will come to a steep rocky notch with two options just ahead: left side or suicide, a clear choice.

The minor top after this notch marks the end of the really difficult stretch. After it continue along the crest to meet a wide, eroded path. You can of course take it but it's preferable to keep to the crest and enjoy excellent views on both sides.

The rule from here on until you hit a track is 'direction north-east'. Take the vague and unravelling path through rocky country, cross a ruined wall, climb a fence, all the time continuing roughly north-east. After which you will reach a track heading, you've guessed it, north-east. The track, evading a farm at one point by diverting right onto a well-constructed path, reaches a narrow road where you turn left to reach the A5 again. After which the car park is just down to the right ■

ROUTE 26: CNICHT FROM CROESOR

Cnicht (689m) is that most distinctive triangular-shaped mountain to the south-east of the main mountain area. A memorable walk to the summit is followed by a duller and navigationally difficult centre section and a scenic return high above a long straight hill valley.

Know Before You Go The centre section of the walk from the summit ridge of Cnicht is quite difficult navigationally but the terrain and eventual target allow a wide margin of error. There is a little simple scrambling. There is not much scope for shortening this walk but you can combine it with Route 27 to lengthen it.

Getting There The start is in the village of Croesor (gr 6344) just off OS sheet 115. Take the A498/A4085 for 5 miles south of Beddgelert, turn left (signposted) and drive for over 2 miles to the village. This is a narrow road so please do not take too many cars. Parking is free but you can support the local community by patronising the charming tearooms in the village. **Bus**: you *could* try the very infrequent 98 service to Croesor.

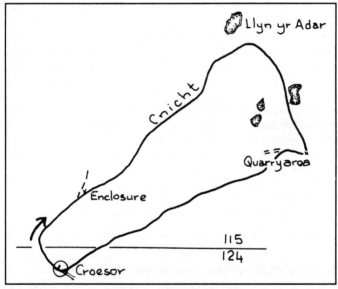

Walking Time 3.5 hours (distance 10km, climb 600m).

Map Strictly both 1:50 000 sheets 115 and 124 are needed but the latter covers such a small part of the route that it might be dispensed with rather than buy it specially for this walk.

Route From the car park turn right, walk up the hill and into a wood and at its end branch right onto a stony track. Don't amble along regardless! After 10 minutes or so along the track look out for a **ruined enclosure** beside it and fork right onto a path to cross the nearby stile.

From here to the summit ridge of Cnicht the scenery is magnificent: rough mountain country diversified by stern, bare, rocky outcrops. Navigation is easy:

keep to the path, which runs mainly along the crest of the spur. At one point you have to skirt the left side of a rocky knoll but after that normal operations resume to the point where you are crossing a tiny grassy plateau about 30m long beyond which is the slightly intimidating steep rocky climb to the summit.

Not to worry. Take the path most of the way and where it disappears scramble over the rocks. From the summit (689m) a lovely panorama awaits with Moel Hebog to the west, and the Snowdon massif and the Glyderau off to the north-west and north.

Now, back to navigation. Continue north-east along the increasingly indistinct summit ridge and then follow a path into not over exciting bogland with the sizable Llyn yr Adar off to the left - its island clearly identifies it. After about 1.5km from the main summit (and you are now at about gr 657477) watch out for a cairn with much more diameter than height, so to speak, and turn right here onto a clear path - a clear path initially, that is.

The target here is the **quarry area** holding a complex of desolate quarry buildings and spoil at gr 665463, and the bearing is about 150° to reach this quite extensive, and therefore easy to find, landmark. Before it is a terrain of bogland, lakes, and rocky outcrops, where the initial clear path degenerates into sub-paths, aspirant paths and decoy paths, so you would be better off working from the compass when the clear path runs out. Incidentally if you find yourself between a large lake on the left and two smaller ones on the right you are pretty well on course.

From the quarry area take the tramway heading initially north-west from its south-west corner *but only for 200m or so.* Then divert left off it to follow a rocky path heading steeply downhill and then on a gently downward trajectory high above Cwm Croesor, a steep-sided, narrow valley with an unusually flat, cultivated floor. A most enjoyable stretch.

At length a signpost will direct you into a field and to an invisible right of way which runs a little to the left of a house and graduates to a track and then a road. From here on it is only a matter of following your nose into the village ■

ROUTE 27: MOELWYN MAWR AND BACH

A short walk with constantly changing views and underfoot conditions but with also some unwelcome man-made constructions notably the remains of mine workings. The walk first rises along the side of pleasant Cwm Croesor, then climbs two partly rocky peaks and finishes with an easy ramble with views to the sea and over a broad lowland valley.

Know Before You Go You will have to have 1:50 000 sheet 124 for this route as well as sheet 115. Take navigational care at the start as the route is a little complicated. The unfortunate non-overlap of the two 1:50 000 sheets makes navigation both at the start and later on a little more difficult.

Getting There Park in the car park in the village of Croesor (gr 6344) as in Route 26 (note the caution).

Walking Time 3.75 hours (distance 10km, climb 700m). **Route** Leave the car park by a footbridge over a stream, turn right and carefully follow a path on the other side (it is not over-clear) to a right angle bend in a track. Turn right here onto the track, walk to the nearby crossroads and turn

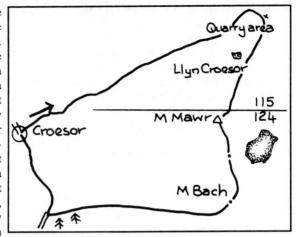

left to keep on the level (do not follow the rising track ahead). Continue along the valley floor and after the house Banc y Moelwyn turn right onto a path rising diagonally left across the slope. Relax navigationally for a while.

This path takes you on a gradually upward path above the long straight valley floor of Cwm Croesor, with good views down and across the valley to Cnicht. At length the path curves left at the head of the valley and joins an old tramway. Turn right onto it and walk to the nearby **quarry area** and extensive ruins at gr 665463, which boasts an odd ladder stile seemingly designed for agile monkeys.

Now for Moelwyn Mawr (770m). The bearing for it is 210° (it's back on sheet 124 and so difficult to figure out) but to start you should walk a little to the left of this bearing to avoid a marshy area around Llyn Croesor. Beyond the lake climb a rocky subsidiary peak and then walk round the rim of a half-hearted corrie to the trig pillar on the summit.

The descent toward Moelwyn Bach to the south is grassy initially but then assumes a steep zig-zag path through rocky ground. It drops into a shallow bwlch, beyond which and nearby is a rocky peak *that is not Moelwyn Bach* but merely a subsidiary top. From this top descend steeply, the ugly Llyn Stwlan Reservoir on the left, to a narrow bwlch where you can easily cut the route short. However, if you want to continue, the climb to the modest cairn on Moelwyn Bach (710m) is straightforward and rewarding.

From Moelwyn Bach follow the broad, grassy crest of the spur westward into increasingly boggy ground and so reach the right side of a block of forest. Take the right of way along the forest edge to a minor road where unsurprisingly you turn right and follow it, via a few gates that should be left as you found them, down into Croesor.

Combination of Routes 26 and 27 These routes can be easily combined giving a walking time of about 4.75 hours (distance 12km, climb 980m) ∎

ROUTE 28: CNICHT FROM BETHANIA

A test of navigation over a varied terrain of bogland, lake and crag, with long stretches without clear paths. The reward consists of excellent views from the long ridge before and after the one summit on the route, Cnicht (689m), and the satisfaction of exploring a remote and challenging area.

Know Before You Go Because of the difficult navigation over much of this route do not attempt it if the visibility is likely to be bad, though a short cut (see below) reduces navigational problems. The road to the starting point is extremely narrow so please minimise the number of cars.

Getting There The start is at the informal car park at gr 632483. To get there on the A498 from Beddgelert turn right at a junction (Bethania on the map but unsignposted) under 3 miles from the town. From the opposite direction, turn left a mile or so beyond the youth hostel. In both cases turn left shortly at the tee and drive less than 2 miles to the car park on the left. **Bus**: Not really feasible. Try the infrequent S97 service from Beddgelert or Betws-y-coed, though this still involves a walk of 3km to the start.

Walking Time 4 hours (distance 10km, climb 660m) including about an extra half-hour for navigational complexities.

Route Walk a few metres farther along the road and turn left over a bridge. Take the clear path beyond it along a stream up into a wild upland valley adorned with lots of crags especially on the right. Continue south as the path levels off, becomes intermittent and descends a little to pass by the shore of an unnamed lake about 100m long in gr 6346. (By the way you can shorten the walk by heading directly from the highest point on the path to the small plateau just south-west of Cnicht's summit.) Beyond the lake, and you are still dropping though the path is now clearer and following another stream, look out on the left for a curious

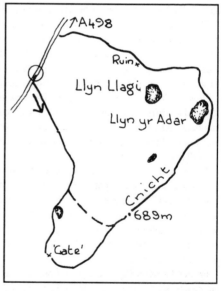

stone 'gate' consisting of five horizontal slabs (gr 635461). This is the point where you should turn off the path and tackle the grassy spur looming just beyond the wall and a little farther on.

To do this cross the 'gate', turn right immediately and follow the wall until you can easily gain the spur and head south-east directly up its crest. When confronted by a craggy cliff at its top, cross a stile just before the cliff and *turn left slightly downhill*. This will allow you to circumvent the craggy area and so reach the crest of the spur. This is Cnicht's south-west extension, and a superb eyrie with the deep trench of Cwm Croesor way down below you and Moelwyn Bach and Mawr beyond it.

Now for Cnicht itself. Head north-east along a clear path running along the crest and when you have crossed a tiny grassy plateau make sure you keep to the steep path just to the right of the crest of the spur and ending in Cnicht (689m) itself.

Correction: ending on the rocky, hummocky crest extending for nearly a kilometre that constitutes Cnicht and whose indeterminate summit does not make route finding any easier. Anyway continue north-east along the crest on a path of sorts until you espy, off to the left, Llyn yr Adar, a desolate, undistinguished lake in a desolate soggy area, harbouring an island which unfortunately doesn't do much to lift the air of desolation.

Never mind. Head for the far (northern) end of the lake and just before you reach its outlet stream head north up through a shallow bwlch. *Do not attempt to follow the outlet stream down* – you will see why later on.

Beyond the bwlch a clear path develops over steeply descending ground. It heads north for a few hundred metres and then swings abruptly left valley-ward into easier ground. As you descend you will see off to the left the impressive Llyn Llagi with a cascade plunging into it – the outlet stream from Llyn yr Adar and certainly not a feasible descent route.

Around here your path takes a somewhat cavalier approach to guiding you: it becomes intermittent with numerous diversionary sub-paths. While it is easy enough to amble westward you are going to have to reach a specific point in the lowlands ahead and to find it you must pick up the path again, specifically at a **ruin with a standing stone** to its right at gr 646486.

From here continue down to cross a stile over a wall, after which the path again becomes quite indistinct. However if in doubt keep the main stream in the valley on the left and head down through crags, grass, bog and scattered trees.

At length you will approach a house at gr 637489. Cross a gate on the house's right, ignore a tempting driveway on the right and pass the front of the house to cross another gate and reach a right of way beyond it. Just before you reach a second house turn right uphill, still on a right of way, to reach tarmac. Turn left for the nearby start ■

ROUTE 29: MOEL DRUMAN AND LLYN EDNO

A walk through a kaleidoscopically varied terrain in a remote area. A hummocky ridge with numerous lakes and several rocky knolls ends at large Llyn Edno from where a clear but difficult path leads down to a shallow bwlch. Then follows in turn a descent through an upland valley, a series of roads, paths and tracks through fields and woods and finally windswept moorland.

Know Before You Go If an all too prolonged view of what appears to be the largest open-cast mine in the world offends you do not go on this walk, or take evasive action (briefly described below). Navigation: though there are several helpful pointers along the route this is a remote area with lots of pathless ground so take care.

Getting There Park in the car park on the A470 just north of the crest of the Crimea Pass (gr 7048) a few miles north of Blaenau Ffestiniog and 9 miles south-west of Betws-y-coed.

Walking Time 5.5 hours (distance 17km, climb 700m).

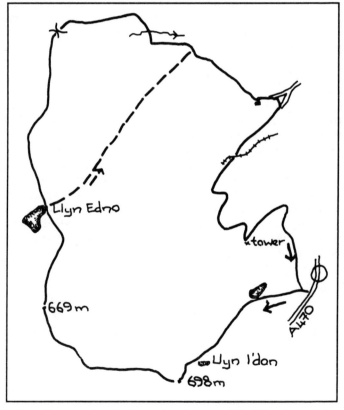

Route From the car park walk the road to the crest of the hill and turn right onto a track. Leave it immediately and take to the high ground running west and overlooking the aforementioned mine. (If you want to postpone the sight of this mine keep to the right of the spur and aim for the south of the lake in gr 6948.) As you advance you will pass under a power line beyond which the crest of the high ground gradually becomes more definite until, with the tiny reservoir (two dams) of Llyn Iwerddon far down on the left you face the one prolonged climb of the day, that to summit 698m, which marks the eastern end of high ground.

There is little point in trying to enumerate all the features now to be encountered on the easy stroll initially west, an area collectively called Moel Druman. Suffice to say that it is an unexpectedly delightful area of knolls, lakes of various dispositions and sizes, scree slopes and slate splinters all the way to the obvious 1m high cairn on summit 669m over two kilometres away. Before you start however a navigational pointer: after summit 698m a fence meanders in from the left and it might be prudent to keep it in sight all the way to far-off Llyn Edno, first as it heads west and then swings north.

After summit 669m the underfoot terrain is more conventional – rough ground and rocky hillocks – but the views, with the Snowdon massif dominating the western horizon, are magnificent all the way to the soggy ground close to Llyn Edno, a large and remote one with a wall of crags on its far shore.

At Llyn Edno you can shorten the route by heading north-east over the rough ground of Yr Arddu to pick up the main route again at a clear track. For the main route follow a clear path north along the right of a ridge of rocky ground reaching most of the way to distant Moel Siabod. Not the easiest of paths, with rock steps and two exceedingly boggy areas to circumvent. You will therefore probably be relieved to reach the shallow Bwlch y Rhediad and face the varied terrain and underfoot conditions back to the start.

The bwlch is the place where I must resort exclusively to tedious directions, since from here on you are going to have to pay attention to navigation.

Turn right over a stile just beyond the lowest point in the bwlch, walk on a path to a clump of trees about a kilometre away, turn right downhill just beyond them to cross the main stream in the valley, turn left to take the track beyond down to civilisation in the form of a farmhouse. Take the road beyond the farmhouse for a few hundred metres and when you see another road far down on the right walk to it and turn right. Stage one over.

The road very shortly becomes a track, passes through a farmyard and, a little beyond this, where you are within a few metres of a railway arch on the left, pass under the arch, turn right and take the path beyond up into a terrain of upland fields diversified by the occasional copse and individual tree, a terrain that unfortunately eventually degenerates into rough moorland. At a well-built **tower**, a vent from the rail tunnel below, swing acutely left onto a track (this change of direction is not self-evident) and take it all the way back to the A470 with the start just to the left ■

TWO WALKING TOURS

Here are two walking tours overnighting in youth hostels. The first is a six-day loop starting and finishing in Bethesda; the second is a five-day A to B route, which is the same as the first for three days but ends up at Nebo to the west.

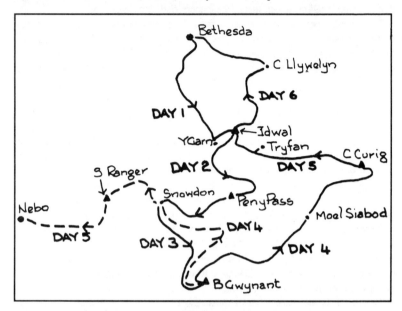

Day 1: This is Route 9. From Bethesda along the west side of Nant Ffrancon, climb Y Garn and down to **Idwal Hostel**. Note that meals are not served here as they are in other hostels on this tour but there is a store which means you can prepare simple meals (but check beforehand). Distance 10km, climb 980m. Bad weather route along the cycleway starting near Bethesda.

Day 2: From the hostel take the obvious path south to Llyn Idwal and from here continue south up the Devil's Kitchen on a steep, made path to near Llyn y Cwn. Then follow Route 10 to **Pen-y-Pass Hostel**. Distance 10km, climb 800m.

Day 3: Take the Miners' or Pyg Track to Snowdon, walk south to the bwlch at gr 605522 on a mostly clear path. Then descend east to **Bryn Gwynant Hostel**, where the end of Route 16 might be some help. Distance 12km, climb 750m.

Bad weather route on the footpath south-east from the hostel, along the upper valley of Afon Glaslyn and on a path above the cliffs on the west side of Llyn Gwynant.

Day 4: Follow the bad weather route (next paragraph) past Llyn Gwynant, walk to the start of Route 24 and follow it to the summit of Moel Siabod. Then follow Route 25 to near the A5, here follow a footpath to **Capel Curig Hostel**. Distance 15km, climb 960m.

In bad weather turn left from the hostel, cross the first footbridge on the right and walk on a path above the cliffs on the west shore of Llyn Gwynant. Descend again to the lake and then take a path to the electricity works at gr 653540. Here follow a track to Pen-y-Gwryd. After that, unfortunately, there is no easy way to Capel Curig – both sides of the A4086 being difficult to walk. Maybe you should have a leisurely drink at Pen-y-Gwryd and then take the bus.

Day 5: This is the start of Route 11, then the second half of Route 8. Capel Curig west to Llyn Caseg-fraith, Bwlch Tryfan, Tryfan, Llyn Bochlwyd and thence to **Idwal Hostel**. Distance 10km, climb 900m. Bad weather route along the valley floor south of the A5.

Day 6: This is the start of Route 1 and the end of Route 2. Pen yr Ole Wen, the High Carneddau and back to **Bethesda.** Distance 15km, climb 1000m. Bad weather route along the cycleway to near Bethesda – hopefully not for the second time.

Nebo-ending Day 4: Bryn Gwynant Hostel to Snowdon as in Route 16 and then the Snowdon Ranger Path to **Snowdon Ranger Hostel**. Distance 16km, climb 1200m, though this route can readily be shortened eg by taking the Watkin Path.

Nebo-ending Day 5: Walk to near Rhyd-Ddu and then follow Route 19. Walk to Nebo for the bus. Distance 16km, climb 1040m.

BAD WEATHER ROUTES

'There's no such thing as bad weather, only bad clothing'. Rarely has such nonsense been seriously promulgated. With rain dripping remorselessly from the trees, cobwebs etched in beads of raindrops, mournful cloud blanketing even the lower hills, who cannot feel a lowering of spirits? But do not despair: it is still possible to get out walking and, who knows, you might even enjoy it.

Here are a few suggestions for bad days. Some of these routes are A to B so either you will have to have a second car at the end or else use the bus service to return. You can avoid the anxiety of possibly missing the bus (or misreading the timetable) by taking the bus before walking, but you may still have to depend on the bus if you decide to cut the route short. It's a difficult call.

If it's really dreadful weather you might consider forest areas, but remember that forests are all too easy to get completely lost in. The best of these are around Betws-y-coed or Beddgelert or you might try the Newborough area in Anglesey, a variation on Route A below.

A: NEWBOROUGH WARREN AREA
A varied walk mostly along the coast to the highlight, the church on Llanddwyn Island (in fact it's a peninsula), with a return maybe through forest. This walk can be up to 18km long but with little climbing as the highest point is barely above sea level.

Park near the village of Newborough in Anglesey at one of the car parks in gr 4264 or gr 4364. Walk out to Abermenai Point (watch out for the tides) and then along the shore west to the church on Llanddwyn. Return through or along the side of Newborough Forest. Most of the route is on the map 115 (the same as for Snowdonia) and although Llanddwyn is just off it you don't need one to reach it.

B: BEDDGELERT AND NANTGWYNANT

A gradually ascending walk through woods and along two lakes overlooked by stern craggy mountain slopes. The start at Beddgelert is about 40m high and Pen-y-Gwryd is about 280m, though you do not have to go so far. A bus or second car is required. The whole walk is 12km long with less than 300m climbing.

From the village walk mostly on path along the east side of Llyn Dinas. Take the A498 for less than 1km and then cross the river by a footbridge to walk along the cliffs above the west side of Llyn Gwynant (there's more about this section under Day 4 of 'Two Walking Tours' on p60). Keep on this side of the valley to the electricity works and then walk back to the A498 by taking a minor road either north to Pen-y-Gwryd or south towards Bryn Gwynant Hostel. Take the infrequent S97 bus back to Beddgelert.

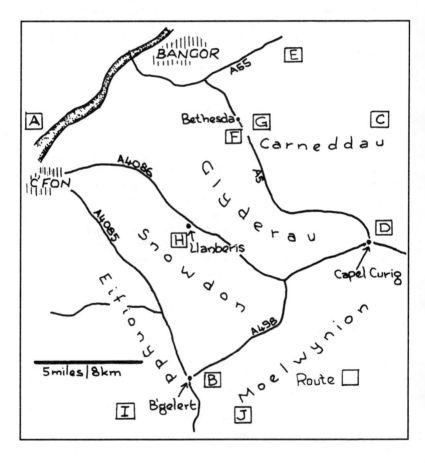

C: CWM EIGIAU

A walk into the remote recesses of Cwm Eigiau, passing the breached dam and farther on past old mine workings with the rocky fastnesses of the Carneddau particularly impressive on the left. The start is at 370m and there is a gradual climb. You can go as far as you like but will have to return by the same route. (You can also explore the valley of the Afon Dulyn.)

The route is the valley section of Route 6.

D: CAPEL CURIG TO LLANRWST

A walk on path through stern, craggy country, along the wooded shores of Llyn Crafnant and then on pleasant, mostly minor roads and across a flat valley to Llanwrst. The highest point is at a pass (340m). The whole walk is 12km long with less than 200m climbing. If the weather clears you might consider walking Route 3.

Take the Capel Curig start of Route 3 to walk over the pass to Llyn Crafnant. Take a minor road down to Trefriw and then a path to Llanrwst. Here take the train or bus to Betws-y-coed and the bus to Capel Curig (check times carefully).

E: THE ABER FALLS AREA

On track through moorland to Llyn Anafon, nestled in a mountain valley, with a variation on the return. The highest point of the route is at 500m. In all 12km with a climb of 500m. If the weather clears you could climb to the bwlch near Pen Bryn-du and take a track or the mountain ridge back to the car park.

Start in the village of Abergwyngregyn (gr 6572) where there is parking just off the A55. (If you prefer to avoid a road walk, even a pleasant one, start in the informal car park at the end of the road (gr 676716)). For the start in the village keep on tarmac to this car park and here take the track to Llyn Anafon. For the return, branch off the track at any convenient point and keep to the river on a rough path all the way back to the car park.

F: BETHESDA TO IDWAL COTTAGE OR CAPEL CURIG

An easy gradually rising track to Idwal Cottage (gr 6460) and a rougher path some of the way past Llyn Ogwen down to Capel Curig. This route is along a wild mountain valley somewhat subdued by carrying a main road. The highest point of this route is about 300m at Idwal Cottage. The distance is about 16km (7km to Idwal) with a climb of about 150m.

Walk south from Bethesda to take the cycleway along the west side of Nant Ffrancon as far as Idwal Cottage. Here cross over to the north side of Llyn Ogwen, walk its length and cross back over the A5 to walk mostly track to Capel Curig. You can get the S6 bus back from Capel Curig or Idwal Cottage or indeed at any intermediate point as long as the bus can safely stop.

G: BETHESDA TO AFON LLAFAR VALLEY

A there-and-back walk into the recesses of a remote, narrow mountain valley nestling between the two highest Carneddau. The highest point is over 500m near the head of the valley; much of the route is sheltered from the prevailing south-west wind. The total distance is about 11km and the climb up to 350m.

As in Route 2 but keep to the valley floor.

H: LLANBERIS TO AFON ARDDU

A walk on track or path into a mountain valley south of Llanberis with the possibility of returning on a partly different route. If you reach the pass at 467m the distance is about 9km in all.

From Llanberis walk past the youth hostel and then south into the sub-valley of the valley carrying Afon Arddu, maybe reaching the pass at 467m. You could return via Hebron Station on the east side of Afon Arddu. Route 15 might be some help.

I: CWM PENNANT

A loop in the partly wooded valley of Pennant with rural road to start, then a touch of mining architecture and ending with a path high above the valley. A lovely walk when the trees are in their autumn colours. The total distance is 9km with a climb of 150m. The highest point is 250m.

Drive the A487 south of Caernarfon and turn left at the sign 'Cwm Pennant'. Cross a bridge after 2.2 miles and then find a considerate parking place either here or a little farther up around a former church.

From the bridge walk to the church, turn left, fork left and keep ambling for scenic miles to the end of tarmac. Here cross the bridge on the right (not the slab bridge), immediately cross a stile, take a right of way rightwards and uphill to a ruined house and beyond it to a substantial stone building from the quarrying era. Just beyond it pick up a track contouring above Cwm Pennant, turn right and walk it for more scenic miles until confronted by a barbed-wire fence. Turn right here to the nearby farm, Cwrt Isaf, and walk back to the start.

J: CWM CROESOR

A walk along a minor road in a remarkably straight and level valley hemmed in by high hills with a return higher up along the valley's side. In essence quite similar to the previous route but convenient if you are coming from the south. The total distance is 6km with a climb of 150m and the highest point is 350m.

Initially follow Route 27 but keep to the valley floor by walking straight on at the right angle bend in the track. Walk to the end of tarmac. Continue on a track for a short distance and then climb directly to a path (the return path for Route 26). Turn right for Croesor.